THE FUNHOUSE MIRROR

THE FUNHOUSE MIRROR

Reflections on Prison

Robert Ellis Gordon
and Inmates of the
Washington Corrections System

Washington State University Press
Pullman, Washington

Washington State
SS University

Washington State University Press
PO Box 645910
Pullman, WA 99164-5910
Phone: 800-354-7360
Fax: 509-335-8568
E-mail: wsupress@wsu.edu
Web site: www.wsu.edu/wsupress

Library of Congress Cataloging-in-Publication Data

Gordon, Robert Ellis, 1954–
    The funhouse mirror : reflections on prison / by Robert Ellis Gordon
and inmates of the Washington corrections system.
        p. cm.
    ISBN 0-87422-198-6 (pbk.)
    1. Prisoners—Washington (State) 2. Correctional personnel—Wash-
ington (State) 3. Prisons—Washington (State) 4. Prisoners' writings,
American. I. Title.

HV9475.W2 G67 2000
365'.44'092—dc21
    [B]   00-022352

Contents

This book is dedicated to the memory
of Kenneth Bernard Schwartz

1954–1995

With the exception of several short stories, this is a work of non-fiction. However, in the interests of privacy, one inmate-author has chosen to write under an assumed name. In addition, to eliminate the possibility of administrative retribution, I have changed the names of several former students. I have also withheld the names of a number of prison staff members who were, at some risk to their job security, extremely helpful and forthcoming with me. For these same reasons, I have, in a very few instances, altered the name of the prison where a particular event occurred. This having been said, all of the events recounted in *The Funhouse Mirror* did, indeed, take place.

Fantasy abandoned by reason produces impossible monsters; united with her she is the mother of the arts and the origin of their marvels.
—Goya

Man in the Cook County Jail being strapped into the electric chair: "This will certainly teach me a lesson."
—Source unknown

Acknowledgments

I WISH TO EXPRESS MY GRATITUDE to my literary agent, Damaris Rowland, for her sound literary advice, extraordinary patience, and unwavering encouragement.

I wish to thank my editor, Keith Petersen, for his encouragement, his wisdom, and his willingness (not that I gave him much choice) to put up with the most obsessive writer in the history of western letters.

I am very thankful for the generosity of Carol Schwartz, Ellen Cohen, Mark and Joan Gordon, and Deborah and Robert Litt.

I am grateful, as always, for the encouragement and incisive editorial advice provided by my close friend and colleague, Thomas Lee Wright.

I wish to express my gratitude to the Washington State Department of Corrections for providing me with the opportunity to teach inside the prisons. I wish to thank the Washington State Arts Commission, the Department of Corrections, and the inmates themselves for funding my teaching programs (through the Inmate Betterment Funds).

I wish to thank the many inmate-students who have chosen to study with me over the years. They are the hungriest, most eager students I have ever had, and they have taught me a great deal about good, evil, truth, lies, suffering, courage, and grace.

Finally, on behalf of my family and myself, I wish to thank Drs. David Tauben and Steven Overman for saving my life during the fall of 1998; for keeping me alive long enough to finish this book (and, with good fortune, for finishing another). A special thanks to Christina Brown, R.N. B.S.N., for her warmth, competence, and seemingly endless supply of compassion.

Introduction

by Robert Ellis Gordon

In March 1989, I taught the first of what was to become a nine-year string of intensive fiction writing workshops in the Washington State prisons. My initiation class was held at the Twin Rivers Correctional Center, one of four prisons situated in Monroe, Washington, a city of 5,300 that lies some thirty-five miles north and east of Seattle in the fertile Skykomish Valley.

On clear days, the horizon to the east of Monroe is broken by the ragged snow-capped ridge of the North Cascade mountain range. On cloudy days, which occur frequently on the west side of the range, the nearby mountains are often but not always shrouded. The weather is fickle in the Pacific Northwest, and its rains are typically gentle, misty, stop-start affairs during which fleeting sun breaks and even rainbows are not uncommon.

As you might expect, this is farm country. If you pay a visit to the Monroe Chamber of Commerce, the employees will, before you get around to asking, or even thinking of asking, cheerfully identify the major agricultural players. (This good cheer, by the way, does not extend to the apparently indelicate topic of Monroe's prisons. You will have to ask questions to acquire information about them, and very specific questions at that. And you may have to answer a few questions about why you're asking.)

But to return to the subject of agriculture: the Chamber people will tell you that it is corn, berry, and dairy farms that drive the rural sector of the local economy. And that is useful information in its way. Still, to a city dweller such as myself, the particular crops and livestock that thrive in Monroe's rolling green fields seem far less significant than does the pervasive fecundity of the place. Things grow in this temperate climate; things grow in this rich, glacial soil. Things grow here because they are meant to grow here, because that is the nature of the land. Or, to put it another way, it would require a great deal of pavement and a great deal of poison to make this valley infertile. If one were serious about the business of preventing growth here, one would have to introduce something quite terrible.

Which leads me, if somewhat indirectly, to those three high security prisons that sit atop the big hill overlooking town. (Monroe's fourth prison, a minimum security farm, is located five miles south of the hard-core joints out on State Route 203.) I hedge with the word "indirectly" because it is not, after all, the purpose of these prisons to prevent growth, at least not in the abrupt sense of the term that comes to mind when one thinks, say, of defoliants, or, for that matter, of the gallows that are still being used to service Washington's very exclusive eight-man death row, more than 300 miles away at the Penitentiary in Walla Walla.

Still, if the phrase "growth prevention" appears in no mission statement put forth by the Department of Corrections, there is nothing about these prisons on the hill that brings to mind words such as nurture or cultivate or fecund. Even good seeds don't flourish in concrete soil or in wild emotional weather. So it stands to reason that bad seeds who inhabit a toxic greenhouse tend not to sprout up in a vibrant, predictable, and dignified manner, but rather to twist, contort, and fester. Except, that is, on those occasions when they do the opposite. Sometimes, in a burst of light and grace that defies common wisdom, that defies everything we think we know about anything, a rage-infested convict will suddenly blossom, dazzling everyone around him with his equanimity. But no one knows why or when these desert flowers will appear, or if they're likely to put down roots or blow away.

So perhaps, after all, this whole metaphor about growth and its prevention won't stand. Perhaps a more inclusive metaphor would be less likely to collapse under the weight of its own exceptions. Perhaps, therefore, a more apt metaphor would be that of a reflecting pool, albeit one we prefer not to look into. Yes, prisons are simply mirrors of what we don't want to see, the funhouse mirrors of the American soul.

Of course, a prison is more than a metaphor. It's an actual place where real events happen every minute of every hour of every day. When you think about a prison in this respect, it can be viewed as the sum total of countless stories.

Here is a story I remember. It occurred at one of those prisons on the hill. It seems that a certain instructor was in the habit of leaving his classroom to use the men's room. When this practice came to the attention of an administrator, the administrator concluded that the instructor's temporary absences represented a breach of security, and the administrator issued a memo to the instructor stating that he was not, under any circumstances, to leave his room while class was in session.

The instructor, a veteran of perhaps too many years in the system, responded to the directive in an unconventional, one might even say inventive fashion. One day, during class, he urinated in his room. He took care, I was told, to aim his stream toward empty desks and unoccupied floor space. Indeed, although minor details varied from tale-teller to tale-teller, all accounts were in agreement on that point: the instructor didn't piss on any students.

Nevertheless, the event caused a bit of a stir, and word of the incident quickly spread throughout the institution. Soon it came to the attention of the prison's education director, a kind, articulate, and bureaucratically savvy woman who was known for her steady composure and ability to put out fires. But something happened that day. When she heard the news, or so the story went, she abruptly stood up and left her office. She drove away from the prison and did not return after lunch. She did not come back to work the next day, or the day after that, or on any day ever again. She had, people said, suffered an instantaneous nervous collapse. She had, people said, gone insane.

There are a couple of lessons to be gleaned from this story. The first and most obvious is that people frequently go over the edge in prison, and it is not always the convicts who snap. The second and less obvious lesson is that once the story escaped the confines of the prison where it happened; once it made its way to Jeno's Restaurant, to Dan's Main Street Grill, and to the Ixtapa Restaurant in downtown Monroe; once it spread from staff member to staff member throughout the North Command—well, it really wasn't all that remarkable. To be sure it was a bit on the kinky side, kinky enough, as prison war stories go, to make the rounds for a week, not just a day. But in the context of the toxic greenhouse, of the funhouse mirror, or whatever foul metaphor suits your taste, the incident was curious and regrettable but hardly unimaginable.

This happened, as I say, several years ago. My guess is that the instructor who urinated in his classroom received a written reprimand. But that's only conjecture, and conjecture aside, the last time I inquired about the instructor's employment status, I was told that he was still on the job.

The story of the instructor who urinated in his classroom is not, of course, the only story I know. If you gave me an evening, or better yet a week of evenings, I could tell you many stories about the prisons. And with a little encouragement and perhaps a glass or two of wine, I could transcend the zone of anecdotal reminiscence and enter the realm of vitriolic ranting.

I would rant against the press for sensationalizing crime; against the politicians who garner votes by preying on fear of crime; and against a public that enables the politicians and the press by tending, on this issue, toward hysteria. I would rail against prison bureaucrats who've either grown callous on the job or who never cared about rehabilitation in the first place. And I would bitterly ruminate upon the manner in which we've cruelly, wastefully, consistently, and unforgivably mismanaged these third world countries in our midst.

Take the issue of education. In the late 1980s, the National Institute of Criminal Justice (the research arm of the federal Justice Department) conducted a comprehensive study pertaining to recidivism. The study tracked 105,000 state prisoners throughout the nation during the first few years after their release. The study found that among members of the general prison population, 66 percent were charged with a felony or a serious misdemeanor within three years of their release. However, recidivism rates for those prisoners who voluntarily completed a high school education while incarcerated dropped to 45 percent. For those who completed a two-year college degree while locked up, the rate dropped to 27.5 percent. And convicts who acquired a four-year college degree while in prison reoffended at a rate of 12.5 percent.

This is a dramatic set of statistics, and one that is, or ought to be, as meaningful to governors, state legislators, law enforcement officials, and other policy makers as it is to teachers and social workers. These numbers should carry a great deal of weight for anyone who professes a belief in crime prevention.

Unfortunately, however, there has been no clamor for more and better educational programming. On the contrary, the pendulum has swung the other way. In my home state of Washington, for example, as part of a new "no-frills" approach to incarceration, the community college system within our prisons has been dismantled. Even high school degrees are no longer offered to those convicts who want them.

Sadly, Washington state is not alone. Education programs have been or are being eliminated in state prison systems throughout the nation. This comes in response to a "lock 'em up and throw away the key" sentiment that has swept across the land. Of course, in most cases, the key is not really thrown away. Sooner or later, almost all prisoners are released. Lacking education, which is to say marketable skills, confidence, and an expanded sense of possibilities, it is inevitable that many of these released prisoners—including the ones who would have acquired an education if it had been offered—will return to what they know best: the life of crime. Thus, the polity's desire for vengeance will be fulfilled at the price of public safety.

In 1989, when I started my prison teaching, the State of Washington housed approximately 7,500 convicts. By late 1996, this figure had grown to more than 12,500 convicts, and the rate of expansion was accelerating. Thus, in less than a decade, Washington's prison population will have doubled.

This trend is not anomalous. It is part of a larger national phenomenon. According to the Justice Department, between 1990 and 1995, we built 213 new state and federal prisons in this country. That comes out to an average of thirty-five prisons per year, or almost three new prisons per month. And that figure doesn't include new county jails or juvenile facilities.

The United States has the highest per capita incarceration rate in the free world. More than two million Americans are presently locked up, and the numbers continue to swell.

Yet vast as this subculture is, very little is known about it. Perhaps that is due to the fact that as a society, we've been in no hurry to lay claim to the prisoners in our midst. And perhaps this reluctance to peer into the funhouse mirror explains our apparent inability to address the problems we are doing our best not to see. Whatever the case, it has been my observation that many of our best educated, best intentioned, and most influential citizens are fundamentally clueless when it comes to the matter of our prisons.

I was reminded of this in January 1993 when I came across an op-ed piece written by the nationally syndicated and highly regarded *Boston Globe* columnist, Ellen Goodman. In the column, Goodman lauded then-New York Governor Mario Cuomo for his decision to grant clemency to Jean Harris, owing to her failing health and her "above average behavioral record during her incarceration."

Harris, the former headmistress of an uppercrust private girls' school, was found guilty, in 1981, of second degree murder. Her victim was her longtime lover, Herman Tarnower, the famous Scarsdale Diet doctor. Tarnower was a notorious philanderer, and Goodman excuses or at least attempts to explain Harris's actions by stating that "Jean Harris was every woman who hung onto a relationship by her fingernails while her self-esteem eroded like a crumbling window sill on the 18th floor. She fell into the abyss."

Goodman goes on to say that

> The irony is that Jean Harris became a model prisoner by fighting the prison model. The irony is that she was 'rehabilitated.' Not by the system, but in opposition to it.
>
> "One fights to stay whole in prison," she wrote from her cell. Indeed, the self-esteem that eroded in long years of her destructive relationship with Tarnower was, remarkably, rebuilt in prison's attempt to destroy her.
>
> In one of three books she wrote, Prisoner 81-G-0098 described, in unsparing, unselfpitying detail, the petty tyrannies of "corrections officers." She described the constant humiliation of strip searches, the deadening routines of waiting before as many as 18 locked doors on each walk to and from meals.
>
> "...How do you teach anything to a human being stripped of all personal dignity?" she asked.
>
> Yet, she found an answer. In prison she...became an advocate for reform, organized programs as if it were her school, taught classes for pregnant mothers, worked at the prison's children's center. The old headmistress ran up good marks in the hostile "learning environment." She earned that "above average behavioral record."
>
> ...It's 1993 and time to free Prisoner 81-G-0098.

I have long admired Ellen Goodman's work, but when I came across this column, I was amazed by her naiveté. Did she not realize that the average incarcerated murderer (or bank robber or car thief, for that matter), lacks influential friends in high places? Did she not realize that the average convict is cut off from the world and has no outside apologists or advocates? Did she not realize, in short, that Jean Harris, by virtue of her prominence and upper class status, was shielded from the worst abuses of the prison system as few convicts ever are?

Apparently not. And so, for the first and only time in my life, I fired off a letter to a columnist.

> As one who conducts story writing workshops in prisons, I was glad to encounter at least one journalist who allows for the

possibility of redemption. Nevertheless, your piece raised some questions in my mind. Are you aware, for example, that it is only because of Jean Harris' prominence that she was permitted to buck the system without suffering the sort of retribution that most prisoners who draw attention to themselves endure? Were she simply an unknown felon, her efforts, no matter how well-intentioned, would almost certainly have led to transfers, isolation cells, and an extension, not a commutation, of her sentence. Prison administrators, governors and parole boards have no great love for agitators.

You allude to the three books Jean Harris wrote while she was behind bars. You commend her for exposing the "petty tyrannies" of the system. Do you understand how perilous her literary activities would've been if, like most convicts, she'd been poor and lacking in influential outside advocates? I had one student (since transferred to Colorado) who wrote an article about the institutional obstacles faced by prison writers. Upon hearing of the imminent publication of his essay, he wrote to tell me that he would pay dearly for this. Sure enough, he was subsequently transferred to a psychiatric hospital, to a locked ward where no books or writing implements were permitted.

This happened in Colorado, as I say, but almost anyone who works in the field of corrections would tell you that the story is not surprising, that it could happen almost anywhere.

...Jean Harris did not receive clemency because of her virtue. She received it because her prominence made it possible for her to demonstrate her virtue without catastrophic retribution from the powers that be. Most of the million-plus convicts in America don't have that option, although thousands would exercise it if they were given the chance.

And so forth and so on. I was on a roll.

Though she certainly had the option of dismissing me as a crank, Ellen Goodman chose not to. Instead she sent a brief reply. "You make a good point," she wrote. "I'll try to keep it in mind."

I hope she does try to keep it in mind. And I hope that other columnists and influential thinkers will choose to take an unflinching look into the funhouse mirrors we've created. For the first step toward remedying the disastrous state of our prisons must be an assault on our ignorance about them.

One morning at the Washington State Reformatory, before creative writing workshop had officially begun, some old-timers were reminiscing. They were talking about the State Penitentiary in Walla Walla back in its "Concrete Mama" days. This was during the 1970s when, in theory, prison reform was at its height. In practice this meant that the administration had loosened controls to such an extent that the guards were cowed by the convicts—at least by the toughest, most predatory convicts—and that the predatory convicts, in turn, pretty much had the run of the place.

As you might expect, this state of affairs led to an increase in sexual violence. Every night, bands of predators would roam the tiers, seeking out the young, the weak, and the unprotected. The predatory convicts would drag their victims from their cells and proceed to viciously rape them.

The guards, being outnumbered, frightened, and demoralized, made no effort to stop the practice. To fill the void, a number of the non-predatory convicts banded together to form The Rape Police. The Rape Police also roamed the cell tiers at night, armed with homemade prison weapons (known as shanks) such as sharpened screwdrivers stolen from the wood shop. The Rape Police tried, with limited success, to intercede and prevent rapes from happening.

Being a rape policeman was a noble and dangerous undertaking. Some rape policemen were singled out and murdered by predatory convicts. The murders were usually carried out in a dark sliver of the prison known as Blood Alley. Blood Alley was a blind spot: it was completely hidden from view by the towers. Guards and other prison staff members rarely ventured into the area.

In addition to murder in Blood Alley, rape policemen also had to fear those guards who, out of fear, corruption, or sadism, were in cahoots with the predatory convicts. These guards liked to "arrest" a rape policeman and throw him into the hole for thirty, sixty, or ninety days. If a rape policeman was carrying a shank at the time of his arrest, formal charges were sometimes filed. A few rape policemen who were charged and found guilty in court of carrying a weapon and/or of assault, ended up having time added to their sentences. One to three years was standard. Five to ten years was not unheard of.

As the old-timers reminisced, I wondered if many people on the outside would have sympathy for victims of prison rapes. After all, these are criminals we're dealing with here, none of whom are in prison for jaywalking. All of them have damaged either property or a person, and some of them have destroyed lives. Moreover, known rapists and child molesters are often singled out for rape in prison.

So I wondered: is the gang rape of a rapist less reprehensible, less unjust, than the gang rape, say, of a bank robber? Or, to put the question in bolder relief, is the rape of a rapist quantifiably less evil than the rape of an innocent citizen?

I don't pretend to have the answers to these questions. But I do know that whenever I walk into a prison, I'm hurled into the realm of moral relativism. Good and evil are not as clear cut as they appear from the outside. Moral black and white gives way to gray. And I'm reminded that our convicts—lawbreakers though they be—aren't really all that different from the rest of us.

To be sure, there are a psychotic few who aren't easily recognizable as human. But they are the rare exceptions. And as for the ones who are unmistakably human? When we give voice to the voiceless; when we give souls to formerly anonymous convicts; when we can no longer deny their humanity, we have no choice but to lay claim to them. Even if we abhor their crimes, we still have no choice but to lay claim to them. And if and when we do that—if and when we peer into the funhouse mirror and conclude that our criminals belong to us and that they're made of the same stuff as us—well then we will, in one respect at least, begin, as a society, to grow up.

When people commend me, as they occasionally do, for working in the prisons; when they praise me for my courage and altruism, I strike an "aw-shucks gee-whiz it's really nothing" pose, and try to steer the conversation to other matters.

This isn't a case of false humility. It's not even a case of *true* humility. What it is is a reluctance to fess up, so to speak, to admit I'm addicted to prisons.

It didn't take long for the addiction to set in. By the end of my first week teaching inside, I was hooked on that savage jailhouse energy, which is composed of so many ingredients: hate, gore, utter despair, the ever-present threat of sudden violence, proximity to evil, proximity to grace, and roll upon roll of barbed razor wire that never once failed to turn my knees into jelly, and send a tremor of fear through my vitals. Prison made for one hell of a thrilling psychic rush, and the other world, the workaday world, seemed pale, drab, and boring by comparison.

I guess you might say that I readily succumbed to the lure of jailhouse adrenaline. I was infatuated with prisons. I *craved* them. For like a good, dependable recreational drug, prison teaching made me euphoric.

Yet there was more than adrenaline at work. You see, teaching in prisons enabled me to meet a number of personal needs. Prisons gave me a mission, for one thing. They gave me a chance to nurture my students; a chance to feel useful and admired. And prisons gave me a new set of friends. They were men, like me, who just didn't fit in; men who'd rejected society's norms.

I felt welcomed and comfortable, extraordinarily comfortable, in a room full of violent felons. Granted, I hadn't robbed or raped or shot someone to death, as had my students. Still, wherever I'd been in my peripatetic life—in my life before I stumbled onto prisons—I'd almost always felt out of place. But now, at last, I had found a true home: I was an outcast surrounded by society's worst outcasts, and that made me feel safe and contented.

This was not, of course, the case with my students, who had precious little cause to feel contented. As TJ Granack writes in his "Letter of August 1991," "I live with hundreds of men pronounced dead on arrival, men who aren't sure if the struggle back to life is possible or even worthwhile."

When my students write stories about their pasts or essays about the prison experience, they are, through the act of creating a piece of literature, struggling back to life. They are also running an emotional risk. For the process of reflection is often painful, and it can trigger a serious depression.

This is true for all writers, of course. But here on the outside we have movies and therapists and alcohol and trips to the wilderness. We have methods for forgetting out here. When a convict writer mucks with his demons, however, he runs the risk of awakening despair and having no place to run from it. If the incarcerated writer starts slipping into the abyss, he's in a perilous situation: there are precious few handholds to stop the slide and no soft spots to land on in prison.

I learned this lesson early on in my prison teaching career. I had just started a two-week residency at the McNeil Island Corrections Center. As I was getting ready to leave the institution for the day, one of my students pulled me aside. He pointed out that in my introductory remarks, I had urged the students to look inward and to pay particular attention to painful memories. "Sadness, anger, and trouble often make for the best stories," I'd said, as I'd said in many classrooms before.

And it's true. Good writing is often a process of alchemy in which we transform the raw, sordid stuff of our lives into something that is precious and gleaming.

But getting back to the student who button-holed me: he informed me that he was serving a life sentence. "And you're asking me to wake up," he said. "Do you know what will happen if I wake up? I'm in here for *life*. Do you understand?"

I wasn't quite sure I understood. But I thanked the student for trying to set me straight, and I advised him to do whatever he had to do to keep from "waking up."

A few days later, we workshopped his first story. It was a powerful story about his grandmother. He had clearly flouted his own inner wisdom in the act of composing the piece. Although the story wasn't trite or the least bit sentimental, it was tender and emotionally searing. The student received lots of positive feedback from the other members of class. I was delighted for him.

That evening, in my room at the Motel 6 in grimy South Tacoma, I savored this quiet victory. I was pleased because this student had reaped a reward for taking an emotional risk. I was pleased because he had a new venue: an art form through which he could channel his memories, his loneliness, his fears, perhaps his rage. He had found a safe method for mining his soul, a safe way to "wake up," and I was glad.

The following day, I was surprised and disappointed when he didn't show up for class. Maybe he's sick, I thought. Certainly, in the wake of yesterday's plaudits, he'd want to come back for more. Or so I assumed. But I was wrong. The student never came to class again.

Naturally, I made inquiries about his whereabouts. I kept asking prison staffers about his status. On the day after his story was workshopped, it seems, he refused to come out of his cell. He was in a bad way, I was told. He was curled up in his bunk in the fetal position. He was in a *very* bad way, I was told. So much so that by the time the residency ended, he'd been put on a suicide watch.

To my knowledge, this student was the only student I ever had who became so depressed by the act of writing that he ended up on a suicide watch. But that doesn't mean that my other prison students don't flirt with despair when they write. In order to tell stories with emotional depth, an author must make himself vulnerable. And that's a dangerous business in prison. Yet my students persist in "going for the juice," in generating painfully honest stories and essays. I'm often awed by the courage with which they write. I thank them for showing me that courage. And I thank them, as well, for what they've written. I thank them for telling me where they come from, who they are, and what it's like to be where they are.

The current discourse on crime and punishment in this country is simplistic, fraught with ignorance, and tinged with hysteria. One book won't alter this state of affairs, but it's my hope that it will make a small difference. It's my hope that the writing produced by my students will temper this debate with a dose of reality about criminals. And what, precisely, is that reality? That criminals, for the most part, aren't monsters. A few are, of course, the superstars of crime: Jeffrey Dahmer, Ted Bundy, John Wayne Gacy. But the monsters are the exceptions, not the rule. The majority of criminals are a lot like you and me, and any number of them are redeemable.

Our present system, unfortunately, does little or nothing to redeem our redeemable convicts. We don't offer them a chance to turn around. And that's too bad for us and tragic for them. We're wasting far too many lives in our prisons. And our present "no frills" approach to corrections is nothing more than a recipe for precipitously increasing the rate at which ex-convicts re-offend.

It is my hope that this book, in its own small way, will change the terms of the current debate; that it will counter rampant ignorance and hysteria about our criminals with a measure of common sense.

Prelude
Letter from TJ Granack
August 1991

I WANT TO TELL YOU about a guy in here who lives in the cell next to mine. Elliott is in his early thirties, though it's hard to tell. He's been down a while, about nine years. Same as me. The word is he shot his wife. Or maybe it was his girlfriend. Anyway, after he killed her he turned the weapon on himself. A botched suicide. I can verify his intent because in all my life I have never seen a more fucked up face and neck. A real Picasso nightmare.

There's an ugly puncture the size of a quarter at the base of his throat. The hole is surrounded by ribbons of brown scar tissue. His jaw is hinged all wrong, exaggerated and twisted a half turn too far. His mouth only opens on one side, and then, only an inch. Five or six teeth are all he's got left; the rest were blasted out.

His left cheek is swollen so large it obscures most of that eye, which, I guess, still works. Speaking of eyes, his never stop watering. The sprinkler system just won't shut down. The same is true of his nose: it never stops running. You can hear him blowing out a continuous flow of mucus at all hours of the day or night. It sounds like an amplified moose call. I can wake up at three in the morning to take a leak and within minutes hear that incredible honking sound.

I don't know if he ever really sleeps.

It's common knowledge that Elliott has never once set foot in the prison visiting room. I've never seen him use a telephone or receive anything other than magazines or junk mail. If he has any family or outside friends, they're not around.

But he doesn't seem to be bitter. The fact is, he's one of the kindest, most well-liked men I've ever met. He holds a job of great responsibility in the prison print shop. He is self-sufficient. He never borrows from anyone and, though he's nobody's fool, he's enormously generous to his friends. He doesn't smoke, yet he likes to keep a pack of Camels in the breast pocket of his work shirt in case a buddy needs a fix.

Elliott is not a visitor here. This is his home and as permanent as the scars on his face. This is where he will die.

I'm not telling you this to condone what he did. It must have been pretty horrible given what's left of him from the neck up. But because I am where I am, I'm privileged to see the hidden side of many public tragedies. I live with hundreds of men pronounced dead on arrival; men who aren't sure if the struggle back to life is possible or even worthwhile.

I think about why I'm here a thousand times a day (don't even ask about the nights). All the places and events involved in my crime. Every word, every glance, every color. They all jumble together and run through my mind like some demented video version of *This Is Your Life* on auto repeat. I can be jogging along the wall in the big yard, peeling a stolen orange in my cell, or just see some ad for a product I used to use, like Turtle Wax or Kodak color film. Even the seasons, the subtle changes in the air, can cause my mind to wander back to the events that led up to my imprisonment. They're a part of me I accept, like a missing limb, or growing older. I couldn't forget them if I tried (which I have no intention of doing). Nothing is stronger. Not even you.

And then I look at Elliott. His face, that grotesque pink and purple lump of stitched-together flesh. Every time he combs his hair, runs soapy hands over the deformed contours of his jaw, brushes what's left of his teeth, *drinks* his dinner from a Styrofoam cup, or painfully blows his nose, he's reminded of what he did to himself and to someone he thought he couldn't live without. It must all seem so unnecessary now.

I know it sounds trite and it's certainly too late to say it, but victims have rights. They should be protected, compensated, and cared for in every way possible. That should never be an issue.

And then I think of Elliott. Someone who did everything in his power to die, forced to wake up in a penitentiary for the rest of his life with a face that never gives him a moment's peace.

Now that's punishment, buddy. It makes me feel lucky knowing someday I'll be able to leave prison, walk down any street, and no one will be the wiser. That the worst thing I've ever done in my life won't be permanently and hideously written all over my face.

So I go on. A daily routine of hard physical exercise (I run till I see visions), simple food, lots of water, and writing give my life a modicum of purpose.

My best to Anita and I hope you two enjoyed your trip to the ocean. You needed the break, I know.

I look forward to your next letter. And remember, if it weren't for us villains, there'd be a lot less heroes out there.

All my love,
TJ

1 | Survival

TJ Granack, who was sentenced in 1983 to serve a thirty-year term for first degree attempted murder, was, as one fellow convict remarked, "an aristocrat among us." TJ was poised and witty; articulate and compassionate; and he comported himself with uncommon grace and dignity.

After serving eleven years of his sentence, TJ was paroled. Of the eighteen men paroled with TJ in November 1994, seventeen were re-arrested prior to the end of their probation periods. TJ, however, sailed through his three-year probation without so much as a single infraction. He is currently employed as a bartender.

Owing to TJ's remarkable ability to engender affection and respect among his fellow convicts, I asked him to write the essay that follows, an essay on how to survive in prison. Notwithstanding his stated reluctance to dwell on prison memories, TJ graciously acceded to my request.

Welcome to the Steel Hotel
Survival Tips for Beginners
by TJ Granack

OKAY, SO YOU JUST LOST YOUR CASE. Maybe you took a plea bargain. Whatever. The point is, you've been sentenced. You've turned yourself over to the authorities and you're in the county jail waiting to catch the next chain to the R Units (receiving) where you'll be stripped and shaved and photographed and processed and sent to one of the various prisons in your state.

Naturally, you're scared. You've never been to prison before. You've lost your job, your home, most of your significant relationships, and your dignity. You think things can't get any worse. But they can. Much worse. Though not necessarily so. It all depends on what state you reside in, what prison you're sent to, and what crime you've committed. With luck, you'll endure a terrible time but will, upon your release, still be able to salvage the rest of your life. If you're unlucky, however, you'll endure years and years of cold, demented violence; years of such unspeakable horror that prison and only prison gets crammed into your brain, and you'll end up doing life without parole, even if you're released.

So what's a felon to do? Here are some survival tips that may make your stay less hellish:

1. COMMIT AN HONORABLE CRIME. If you must commit a crime, go about it in a sensible fashion. Commit a crime that's considered, among convicts, to be worthy of respect. Here, in order of honor bequeathed, are the five best crimes to commit:
- Murder One
- All other assault
- Armed robbery (banks are cool)
- Kidnapping (hostages are cool)
- Drugs (drugs are cool)

I was lucky. I went down for first degree attempted murder, so my crime fell into the "honorable" category. Oh, goodie. So I just had to endure the everyday sort of danger and abuse that comes with prison life.

But what if you're not up to killing a human being, and don't feel like robbing a bank? Then at least commit a neutral crime such as arson, burglary, or theft. And whatever you do, don't go to prison for sodomizing a milk cow or having sex with anything under the age of eighteen.

And why, you may ask, is that true? Because, for you, prison is not some place to visit. It's your new home. And the men who surround you are your new neighbors. And they'll want to know who you are and what you did, although specific details aren't usually important. For example, they won't care if you bludgeoned a seventy-nine year old blind woman to death because she wouldn't tell you where she kept a couple of bucks worth of change. What's important is that you're in for second degree aggravated murder. You're at the top of the prison pecking order. You're down on an honorable crime. You've got what in prison jargon is known as "heart." Hell, you're a fucking hero. You'll have little trouble with your fellow cons. You're an officer. You can walk down the tier with your head held high. You were uncontrollably violent. Therefore, you are now respected.

As I said, details aren't generally important. So let's say there's a thirty-two-year-old guy who had consensual sex with his seventeen-year-old baby sitter. He's a sex offender. A rapo. A baby raper. He might as well have had forced sex with a three-year-old boy. A rapo is a rapo no matter what the circumstances. There are no varying grades in this category. And once you get the "rapo" tag you're done for. Everybody, whether they want to or not, will treat you like a pariah at best or, at worst, like a rodent to be kicked, beaten, and, yes, raped. You see, according to jailhouse logic, sodomizing a rapo is fit and appropriate punishment—and this from guys who hate sicko perverts who force sex on the weak and the vulnerable.

Go figure.

2. DON'T GAMBLE. Not cards, not chess, not the Super Bowl. And if you do, don't bet too much. If you lose too much, and pay up (don't even think of doing otherwise unless you're the toughest motherfucker on the tier) then you'll be known as a rich guy who'll be very popular with the vultures. Or worse, you may win too much and have to collect. In which case the guy who owes you may decide it's cheaper to kill you and take all your possessions than it is to pay off the debt. Or, if the guy is weak and unable to pay, he may decide to check in to protective custody (PC) in which case he'll be required to give up a name, and that's you.

3. BE POOR. At least at the start of your sentence. Never talk about money unless you're complaining about being broke. Never buy in large quantities at the commissary. And only wear prison issue clothing. No Member's Only jackets, no Air Jordan's, no flashy jewelry or apparel. If you dress fancy, you'll be asking for trouble. Chances are, at the start of your sentence, you'll stand out anyway—you'll still carry yourself like a civilian. And that means fresh meat to the scores of vultures waiting for a mark like you to parade through the chow hall. So don't draw further attention to yourself. Just put on your oversized state issue coat, put your hands in your pockets, tilt your head down, look at the floor, and keep walking.

4. NEVER LOAN ANYONE ANYTHING. Because if you do, you'll be expected to collect one way or another. If you don't collect, you'll be known as a mark, as someone without enough heart to take back his own. This should be avoided at all costs. Once you're known as weak, you'll have a hell of a time being known otherwise. Word will spread like wild fire that there's a rich mark on the tier with no teeth, no heart. Your personal possessions will be laid out like a garage sale, and you'll have only two options: fight for your stuff or go to the man, snitch off whomever took your stuff, and be prepared to do the rest of your time in PC along with all the other snitches and undesirables too ill equipped to handle the rigors and madness of prison life in the general population.

5. BUY CIGARETTES. Smoking may be on the way out on your side of the walls, but it's still the overwhelming habit of choice in the joint, which makes tobacco the main form of currency. New sheets, fresh fruit, typing paper, instant coffee, peanut butter and jelly sandwiches, a reasonably unsticky copy of *Juggs Magazine*—all can be acquired with a pack or two of smokes. Two or three packs can get you set up when you first arrive at a new prison. Have them in your property. They'll help you get a decent cell, a good laundry man, and a connection with the kitchen clerk so the food on your tray won't have maggots.

6. MAKE NO EYE CONTACT. Don't look anyone in the eye. Ever. Locking eyes with another man, be he a convict or a guard, is considered a challenge, a threat, and should, therefore, be avoided.

7. PICK YOUR FRIENDS CAREFULLY. In prison, you not only have to ride your own beef (crime) but those of your friends', too. So if you are seen with persons of questionable character (see Survival Tip 1 on "honorable crimes"), you'll be cornered in the prison library and asked if you knew your pals were a bunch of rapos and snitches, and, if so, what are you going to do about it. When you choose a friend, someone to walk the Big Yard with, someone to share your table in the chow hall, you've got to be prepared to deal with anything that person may have done. Their reputation is yours, and the consequences can be enormous.

8. FIGHT AND FIGHT DIRTY. You have to fight, and not according to Marquis of Queensbury rules, either. The object is to win, or at least to do enough damage to make any bullies think twice before trying to take your lunch money. If you do it right, you'll only have to do it once or twice. If you don't, expect regular whoopings and loss of possessions. You won't be able to walk out of your cell with a pack of cigarettes without incurring some sort of confrontation with every bully in the joint. You'll get beat up and ripped off every day until you choose to fight back. But by then you'll have a reputation as a weakling, so fighting back may not help your cause.

9. BE UGLY. This is for all you young guys out there, or for any of you who are good looking in the least. Begin by not shaving, unless you're really ugly. If your beard is spotty, so be it. A nice haircut, or even combed hair, is not a good idea. Rough yourself up a bit. You want to look as unappealing and as unapproachable as possible, especially at the start of your sentence, before you've had a chance to establish your reputation as a tough guy whose bootie is not for sale.

10. MIND YOUR OWN BUSINESS. Never get in the middle of anyone else's discussion/argument/confrontation/fight. If you do, you're liable to lose most of your front teeth. Never "burglarize" someone else's conversation. Never offer unsolicited knowledge or advice.

11. KEEP A GOOD PORN COLLECTION. Gotta have one. Gotta brag about it. Gotta share it, even if it's just through the bars for the other cons to see. You gotta have one with red hot babes dripping on every page. If you *don't* have one, the boys will think you're funny, see? And that's not good, because you've got enough problems on your hands without having to deal with the fact that 900 ugly, horny, and violent men heard that you're a funny boy, dig?

12. LEARN TO MASTURBATE QUICKLY. You don't have much time, so concentrate. With a little practice you'll be able to knock one out during door rack (about 3 or 4 minutes). If you've got talent, you can knock out two. Just think about what a wonderful skill this will be when you're released.

13. NEVER EVER LOOK INTO ANOTHER MAN'S CELL. (See Survival Tip 12.) Never look unless you're prepared to see something you don't want to see, and to deal with the consequences of having been seen seeing it. When you enter prison, your world has shrunk, and the little city you now live in is full of activity, most of which you want nothing to do with. Two guys can be fighting or fucking in the cell next to yours, but that's clear across town as far as you're concerned.

14. DON'T TALK TO STAFF, ESPECIALLY GUARDS. Don't talk to anyone in authority for long. You might be tempted to exchange small talk with teachers or staff, with someone you might have had something in common with on the outs. Don't succumb to the temptation. Any prolonged discussions or associations with staff makes you susceptible to rumor and suspicion of being a snitch. And that is to be avoided at all costs.

15. NEVER SNITCH. Or even *appear* to snitch. (See survival tip 14.) If there's a drug or weapon bust on the tier, if the guards break into the laundry room and find ten gallons of pruno (home brewed wine) cooking in garbage bags in a heating shaft, and somebody *thought* they saw you talking to a guard or other staff member before the bust, you'll be suspect. If you get caught looking into someone's cell and that cell gets raided afterwards, you'll be held accountable.

So avoid the appearance of snitching. And above all, avoid the real thing. Never snitch another convict off. It's just not done. And if you do, you'd better not get caught. (You think the guard you snitched to will protect you?)

If you're doing a chunk of time you don't want to spend it all in PC, which is what you'll do if you get labeled a snitch (equal to a rapo but more dangerous according to the convict code of conduct). Your name will be mud throughout the entire prison system. Inmates will rob and beat and ridicule you every chance they get. Even if you're transferred to another prison in the state, you'll be marked. The cons will be waiting for you. And the guards will hate you because they'll have to take care of you. Guards don't like snitches, either. To them you're simply garbage who is ratting off other garbage.

Interlude

Ambiance

by Robert Ellis Gordon

Prisons vary. Even a small child returning from a visit to the penitentiary could tell you if the place where Daddy lives has big tall walls or
no walls at all, or if the guards there carry unholstered rifles,
holstered pistols, or merely pack walkie-talkies.

Here in the State of Washington, there are prisons that are designed with a frontier sense of abundant land; institutions where the
low-slung one and two story buildings are spread out in such a way as
to reveal big skies and horizons without walls, genuine horizons
where the sun really rises and the sun really sets at the visible edges
of the earth. In open range prisons such as these, the smell of indus-
trial kitchens intermingled with the fumes introduced every hour by
a thousand hand-rolled cigarettes smoked down to the nubbin, along
with the many varieties of sweat generated by chronic fear, chronic
hate, bloody memories, rotten childhoods, furious workouts, fester-
ing grudges, dread of rape, desire to rape, boredom, insanity, rage,
despair, and too many unwashed socks—well that familiar prison
odor is washed clean, now and then, by a purgative breeze that car-
ries the crisp, sweet scent of a nearby cedar forest or even of the far
off sea. In open range prisons such as these, one can see inmates and
staff members alike pause on a quiet morning to watch the mist rise
from a tree-studded hillside, or, on an especially felicitous day, to ob-
serve a deer graze, without concern for crime and punishment, on
the grass just beyond the fenced perimeter.

And then there are the prisons that never let you forget; the ones
that are designed with an urban sense of scarce and encroaching
space. That such prisons are invariably located in no one's back yard,
far out in the countryside where there are too few voters to prevent
their construction, is irrelevant. For once you step inside one of these
citified institutions, you have entered a rough, hemmed-in tenement
block where the natural world is either oddly contorted or simply
ceases to exist. Walls, like tall buildings, bend the hours of the day,
delaying sunrise until the morning is well under way, and hastening
the onset of sunset. Blazing quartz lights block out the night sky.
Moon and stars, trees and fields and hills—they quickly become ab-
stract and ungraspable, reference points belonging to others, just
stuff convicts see on TV. Even the big exercise yards in prisons such

as these tend more towards spit-pocked expanses of mud than to green and fragrant grass.

There are maximum, medium, and minimum security prisons. There are prisons for women and prisons for men. There are prisons for boys and for girls. At some prisons, the convicts march in file to work and chow; at others, they amble from all directions. At some prisons the convicts all wear the same clothes: blue denim pants and drab olive work shirts. At others they get to dress up like bikers or rock stars or fierce, bearded, kerchief-crowned pirates, albeit the scabbardless kind.

To reiterate then, prisons vary. But pronounced and obvious as these surface differences are, I think it is only after you have spent a bit of time inside a few institutions that you begin to develop an appreciation for the distinctive varieties of pathology and pain that a particular prison generates.

Granted, there are places where living conditions are so squalid that, with regard to the question of subsurface essence, there is nothing subtle or difficult to ascertain. At the old McNeil Island, for example, eight men and one toilet inhabited barred, open-tiered cells that were considerably smaller than the average household's living room. The cells were stacked four high, four deep, and four across, and they were situated in a filthy, drafty, nineteenth-century monster of a building that my students insisted, to a man, was haunted by many ghosts. One day, after a guard had given me a quick tour of the cell house on my way to class, I asked a student how he managed to survive in such a place.

"Always carry violence in your back pocket," he said, meaning, I presumed, that that was the best and maybe the only method for avoiding shankings and rapes.

"But how do you keep from going crazy?"

The student shrugged and said nothing, though perhaps his tight, scrunched-up body, his ever-darting eyes, and his tendency to get up and pace five or six times an hour had been giving me the answer all along.

2 | Porkchop

In 1988 at the age of eighteen, Michael Collins was sentenced to serve eight years in Washington and ten years in Oregon on five counts of armed robbery.

When Collins first got to the Washington Corrections Center in Shelton, he was scared and with good reason. He was young and handsome, factors that made him a sexually delectable target for any number of his fellow convicts.

When he was transferred to the Washington State Reformatory in Monroe in 1990, Collins was still young and handsome enough to attract the attention of would-be rapists and suitors. In the creative writing workshop where I met Collins, for example, a horny old-timer kept leering and ogling as if, as TJ Granack remarked one day, Collins was "a porkchop with applesauce."

Upon completing his sentence in Washington (with some time off for good behavior), Collins was shipped to Oregon to serve out a sentence there. He was paroled in the summer of 1997, and currently works as a cable installer.

At the time of Collins's release, I had just started to work on a manuscript about the prisons. I asked my ex-student if he'd be willing to write about sex behind the lines. I told him that outsiders such as myself hear lots of horrifying rumors, but very few specifics. Who gets raped and why? How does a "fresh fish" maintain his virginity, or is that an impossibility? And what, precisely, had Collins endured?

This was, maybe, an indelicate request on my part, but Collins agreed to give it a try. He was as good as his word: within a month I received both of the essays that follow.

Seventeen Fist Fights Later

by Michael Collins

N JULY OF 1988, just six weeks after I graduated from high school, I was arrested for five counts of first degree armed robbery. I had committed the robberies in two states, Washington and Oregon. Consequently, I received two sentences: eight years in Washington and ten years in Oregon.

I served my Washington time first. As I was being transported on the chain bus from county jail to state prison, I was, to say the least, very scared. At the age of eighteen, I knew I would be among the youngest inmates in the correctional system. And I'd been warned, several years before, by my Uncle Dale, that I was "too young and pretty" to be messing with the law. Uncle Dale was a wise and very tough ex-con. He'd told me that if I kept up with my criminal ways, the horny convict bulldogs would be playing poker for the privilege of fucking me in the ass just as soon as I arrived in the joint.

Fortunately for me, I was initially sent to the Washington Corrections Center (WCC) in Shelton. WCC was and still is the softest of the medium security prisons in the state. So my uncle's warning notwithstanding, (and scared shitless though I was), nothing terrible happened to me my first day in prison. No group of hairy bikers stood me in the middle of a stainless steel table, me being a lone poker chip in a game of five card low in the hole. Nobody tried to rape me, kill me, or even beat me up. It is true that my first day in prison, a dude a few cells down cut off his testicles with a razor blade and threw them out onto the tier. But that sort of event, I quickly learned, just came with the prison territory.

In addition to being sent to a relatively soft joint, I was fortunate because I was in for armed robbery, a crime which placed me in the upper echelons of the local social strata. I was exempt from the sort of random attacks a known rapist could expect any time he left his cell. I was also lucky because I had gleaned, from various tales and horror stories I'd heard in county jail, the rudiments of the convict code: don't snitch, don't shoot the shit with The Man, and don't even appear to be overhearing (let alone butt into) Psycho and Bubba's conversation on the joys of stuffing balloons packed with heroin up one's ass and smuggling them out of the visiting room.

Still, I was too young and not ugly enough to keep the sharks completely at bay. In order to maintain my virginity, therefore, I took several preventive steps. One was to avoid drugs. Bootie bandits (convicts who are known for pressuring new arrivals—invariably young white ones—into sex), often lure their prey with drugs. The bandit supplies the pretty young fish with weed, or, better yet, gets him strung out on heroin or coke, so that the fish will do *anything* for a fix.

I also avoided gambling of any kind. Bootie bandits like to get fresh fish in debt because when the fish doesn't have enough money to pay up, the bandit takes it out in trade, which is to say in sexual favors.

Finally, I did my best to be a loner, because if you're seen hanging around with the wrong type of people in the joint, you're automatically guilty by association. I especially tried to avoid hanging out with "punks," a punk being another convict's "wife" or "girlfriend."

It's strange, but if a naive young prisoner is seen hanging out with a punk, he is quickly labeled a punk. And once he is labeled a punk, all the bulldogs and bootie bandits who don't have a punk, and/or those who want a new one, race to gaff up and "turn out" this new prospect who is not yet, at this juncture, "owned." And since everyone *knows* this youngster is a punk, since he has so obviously proclaimed his punkhood by hanging out with another punk, efforts to turn and own him are doubled and redoubled.

Well, as I say, being scared and more than a bit paranoid, I was suspicious of anybody who wanted to be my pal (which, at the time, seemed like everybody in the joint). So I didn't make the mistake of hanging out with known punks (or rapos or snitches for that matter). Instead, I made a different mistake: I beat up one of the punks. The reason I did was that this particular punk slipped me a note a few seconds before we were locked down for count one day. In the note he said that he would very much like to, and I quote, "suck you dry." And so, not knowing what else to do, even after having a whole hour to think about it, when the cell doors racked open I walked over and hit the guy several times in the face as hard as I could.

This was, I soon learned, a very big mistake. For when you beat up a punk, what you are really doing is beating up somebody's wife or girlfriend. And sure enough, on the day after I hit the punk, his boyfriend hit me several times in the face as hard as he could. He told me he'd kill me if I ever so much as looked at his bitch. Then he beat up his bitch. Then he beat me up again for trying to beat him up for beating me up.

This went on for quite some time. And it taught me a valuable lesson: when a punk tells you he'd like to suck you dry, just say, "No thanks."

In the months following this incident, I enjoyed some peace. The fact that I had showed some heart, that I would fight (though not very skillfully), left most of the sharks with the impression that they'd have better luck going after other young fish.

But then, one summer morning in 1989, I had another ugly confrontation. It came about as a result of a glitch in prison security. The cell doors had been racked open, just as they would be on any morning, but no guard appeared on the tier. Either a fight had broken out on another tier or there was a medical emergency, I forget which. What is significant is that when the guard finished responding to the call, he went directly to the sergeant's office to write his report, forgetting that he'd racked the doors open. It took less than two minutes for the convicts on the tier to figure out that the guard had messed up. Two more minutes and cells were being looted, and TV's and stereos belonging to enemies, snitches, and rapos were being smashed.

I stood at my cell door, watching. For at least ten minutes grown men ran up and down the tier hollering and giggling. As time moved on, however, activity on the tier diminished. My guess is that half the guys had returned to their cells to stow away stolen items, while the other half had returned to their cells to protect their personal property. And when the melee came almost completely to a halt, creating an uncanny and most unusual (for prison) silence, I looked up and saw a black convict standing in my doorway, and knew I was in deep shit.

I knew I was in deep shit because this dude was reputed to be tough, very tough. He was bigger than I was and he was known to be a big time bootie bandit. He stood there at my door for a minute, one hand in his coat pocket, and looked at me. He looked both ways down the tier, leaned against the doorway, and said nine little choppy words. "Shit on my dick," he said, "or blood on my shank."

He was giving me a choice. I could either let him shove his dick up my ass, or he would stab me with a homemade weapon.

"Fuck you, faggot," I said.

Without another word, the guy walked away and down the tier. I sat there for a moment, knowing that he would come back, and for some reason I untied my shoes and relaced them tightly. As I finished this task and stood up, the bootie bandit came flying into my cell with a shank in his hand. His shank appeared to be a knitting needle (God knows where he got it) with a bunch of tape at the blunt end for a handle. He swung the thing at my face. I was lucky enough to have time to throw up my arm, and I received a stab wound in my forearm.

I stepped back from the bootie bandit, clutching my arm. As I did so, I noticed a Bic pen on my desk. I remember noting it was a blue Bic. I picked it up, and we started exchanging blows, the bandit repeatedly hitting me on the left side of my ribs with the now-bent knitting needle, and me trying to puncture his face with my blue Bic. After exchanging several more blows, we ended up grappling on the floor. Then someone shouted "Guard!" and it was over.

The bootie bandit walked away, back down the tier to his cell. His face was pretty gouged up from my pen, and he never gave me any trouble after that. In fact, for the rest of my stay at WCC, nobody gave me any trouble. My reputation as a fighter was established.

In 1990, I was transferred from WCC to the Washington State Reformatory (WSR) in Monroe. I didn't have a reputation at WSR, and I was still pretty young (only twenty), and not ugly enough to keep the sharks away. So once again I had to fight for my virginity.

Overall, those first few years in prison, I was involved in a total of seventeen fist fights. Consequently, I spent a lot of time in the hole (solitary confinement). I'm not proud of the fact that I was in all those fights. But I'm not ashamed, either. The alternative to fighting was to turn into someone's punk, and that was unacceptable to me.

Epiphany
by Michael Collins

I beat up my first rapist on Christmas Eve of 1988. I don't remember exactly how it all happened; how it started, how I brought myself to do it. But I do remember that I walked up to this person, this unsuspecting man, and hit him.

Maybe he thought he'd make it through the evening without being harassed. Maybe he thought the holiday spirit would give him a reprieve. But if that's what he thought, it was wishful thinking. It's never easy to do time when you are a known sex offender in prison, not even on Christmas Eve.

I can still see the look on his face after I hit him, and as I kept hitting him. And nine years after the event I can still remember the sound of his voice. Not words, just sounds, a series of grunts and a sort of whimpering as he fell to the concrete floor in the dayroom. There were twenty or thirty spectators, watching and cheering me on. Never in my life had it felt so terrible to hit someone, and never had it felt so good.

In the following years, I assaulted a number of sex offenders in the same fashion. Sometimes I'd hit them. Sometimes I'd just spit on them or slap them once or twice. Sometimes I'd get in trouble for it, and sometimes I wouldn't. But I never felt bad about it, not after the first time. I didn't feel anything at all. I beat up sex offenders because it was my right to do so, my right as someone who was in prison for an "honorable crime," mine being armed robbery. Sex offenders are the worst kind of criminals, the only bad kind, really. At least in the context of prison. They are the lowest of the low on the pecking order.

For years, I didn't think about the crimes I'd committed: five robberies, all convenience stores. Even after I was convicted and sentenced, I never thought about the people, almost all of them women, who worked in those stores. I suppose I was too busy figuring out how to get by in prison, and figuring out how to be a smarter and better criminal once I got out.

And then one night, something happened. I turned off my cell light and lay down on my bunk. I was drifting off to sleep when, suddenly, it hit me: a flashback. It didn't feel like a memory. It felt as if I was actually re-experiencing one of my crimes. I wasn't simply remembering: I was *there*. I was in the middle of a robbery, the last one I committed.

I had robbed this same store a week previously and the same clerk stood behind the counter. I handed her a duffel bag without saying a word. And without saying a word she emptied the contents of the cash register into the bag. She knew what to do. What else should she have done when confronted by a customer who was wearing a mask and pointing a .350 Magnum?

As she handed me the bag with the money, a door opened behind me. I spun around and pointed the gun right at the face of a woman who'd just come out of the rest room. She fell to the floor as if I'd struck her. She lay there in the fetal position with her hands in front of her face, trembling and begging me not to shoot her. I must have stood there, frozen, for a few seconds. Then I realized that I was still pointing the gun at her face.

I ran out of the store. I ran, in fact, almost forty miles through the woods that day, running from the police who'd shown up less than a minute after I'd left the store.

I was eighteen years old at that time. I didn't know much about the law; didn't know that armed robbery was considered to be a very serious crime. And I didn't know what I was doing to my victims.

Today, after doing nine years in prison, and having been out almost seven months, I wonder why it took me so long to figure it out, to realize that what I did wasn't very much different than rape.

The woman who walked out of that rest room; the woman who, up to that point, had probably lived a regular life, maybe even a happy one, did not know if she would live or die that day. She didn't know what was going to happen to her, just as surely as a woman who is being raped doesn't know. And, as is the case with a rape victim, the victim of any violent crime can never again feel that he or she inhabits a safe and secure world.

The physical trauma inflicted by a rapist might disappear after a few months, but the emotional scars remain. And the same holds true for that woman on the floor, a woman whom I never even touched.

I figured all this out that night in my cell. I am grateful for that frightening flashback. It changed my outlook on life. Even though I couldn't undo what I'd done—couldn't take back the terror I'd inflicted—I came to understand the brutality of my crimes, and that I was no more virtuous than the rapists I used to beat up with so much relish and frequency.

Interlude

Charity

by Robert Ellis Gordon

It was time for mid-morning count. A guard came into the classroom where the creative writing workshop was being held. It was a female guard. This was not unusual. There were many female guards in the institution.

Still, there was something different about this female guard. She lacked the hard, masculine mannerisms adopted by many of her female colleagues. She wore lots of perfume and made no attempt to hide her curves which, as it so happened, were pronounced. Moreover, as she read off the names on the roster, it appeared to me that she was making eye contact with the men in an unmistakably flirtatious manner.

After count was cleared and the guard left the room, everyone was silent for a bit. The scent of the guard's perfume lingered in the air. Finally, a student spoke. He looked at me and said, "That lady's a stripper. She dances at some strip joint in Seattle."

Another student spoke up. "She works on Tuesday and Wednesday nights. In case you want to go see her."

Then a third student chimed in. He told an incredible story. He said a year or so ago a convict had escaped from the nearby Washington State Reformatory. He said the convict was understandably horny: he hadn't had sex or even seen a naked woman for years. So he went to see some strippers at a strip joint. And wouldn't you know, that particular guard was dancing at that particular strip joint on that particular night. The guard recognized the escapee from the Reformatory. She tipped off a bunch of the customers. "And they pounced on the guy," said the student. "They beat the living shit out of the guy."

I gazed at the student who'd told the story.

"No lie," said the student.

"No lie?"

The student paused and then he smiled. "Her name is Charity."

"Charity?" I said.

"Charity," he said.

I mulled this one over for a bit.

At lunch I told my supervisor the story of Charity, and asked if it was true.

"Yes," said my supervisor. "It's true."

"Even the part about fingering the guy? About the guy getting beat up at the strip joint?"

"Yes," said my supervisor. "It's true."

"It appeared to me," I said, "that she was flirting with the guys."

"She's got a reputation for flirting," said my supervisor.

"But why?" I asked. "Why flirt with these guys? They're romantically unavailable, to put it mildly."

My supervisor was usually a patient man, but on this day he got exasperated. "Can't you recognize a power trip when it's staring you in the face? This place is *twisted*," he said, "fucking *twisted*!"

3 | Rapo

Twice-convicted rapist Duane Eaglestaff is a resident of the Special Commitment Center (SCC), a place where some sex offenders are sent upon completing their prison sentences. In order to be released from the SCC, a resident must prove that he's been cured of deviant urges. In the eight years since the 1990 passage of the Civil Commitment Act, SCC officials have never once recommended that a resident be released.

Prior to his transfer to the Special Commitment Center, Eaglestaff was in an unenviable situation: he was a known sex offender in prison. His account of that experience follows.

A Sex Offender's Account

by Duane Eaglestaff

I N 1976, AT THE AGE OF TWENTY-FIVE, I was sentenced to serve thirty
years for first degree rape. I was initially sent to the Washington
State Reformatory (WSR). From the outside, WSR appeared to be
about as big as a high school football field. It was surrounded by a
huge brick wall.

When we were transported into the institution, many inmates
flocked to the fence to see who was coming in "on the chain." This
was a weekly sporting event.

Once inside WSR, I noticed that the buildings were cracked from
almost a century of wear, and that the paint was urine-yellow. Everything was old and filthy. The place even smelled old. I asked myself
how could I spend the rest of my life here.

My chainmates and I were given clothes and bedding. It was
great to finally get some decent clothes after shivering for months in
the Receiving Units down at the Washington Corrections Center in
Shelton. I could finally get warm under the coat they issued to me. I
was also issued a mattress, bedding, and toothpaste.

"You go to Charlie 4-21," some guy said. I don't know if he was an
inmate or a guard. You couldn't really tell in those days. Security was
loose back then, and inmates, including the most brutal ones, had
free rein to wander about the institution. During my time at WSR, I
saw inmates kill themselves and each other.

I found my "house" and put my load on the bed. I was four stories
in the air on a sidewalk about four feet wide with a railing that came
up to my waist. People were everywhere, wall to wall, shoulder to
shoulder. They were standing on hallways and tiers, and laying down
on hallways and tiers. I was in a human junkyard. Each human wore
their identity: the look-out, the dealer, the killer, the homo. Who was
I? I didn't know. All I knew for certain was that I was scared shitless.

On my first day, a black guy asked me if I wanted to get high. I
said sure. He wanted me to come into his cell. I sensed that he didn't
have any weed in his cell, and that this was some kind of a scam. I
changed my mind and walked away.

On that first day at WSR, I recognized two guys that I had known
from days gone by. These were the only people I recognized out of
about a thousand inmates. One was black and one was white. I told
the black guy what had happened with the weed man. The next day,

Weed Man came up to me and told me that saying stuff to other people would get me killed. Not bad, right? Only two days inside, and I had learned one thing that would get me killed: telling the truth.

A few weeks later, the president of the Lifer's Club wanted to meet with me and talk. The prison psychologist arranged the meeting, and to this day I do not know why. The Lifer and I met in the Doc's office and, being a complete fool, I told the Lifer what I was in for: Rape in the First Degree. I thought I was making a friend when in fact I was simply fulfilling the Lifer's mission of being a prisoner who knows about everybody else. Information is power in prison.

From that point on, everyone in the joint knew what I was down for, and that wasn't good. You see, in prison, everyone knows that they have done something wrong. For this reason, everyone wants to feel better than the guy next to him. Murderers are the most respected prisoners. Maybe it's because their crimes are worse than any other. Sex crimes are classified as the worst in prison. I really do not know why.

So as I say, I was now in peril. But I excelled in sports and that's, maybe, what saved my life. That, and my insistence on standing up for myself every time I was challenged.

With regard to sports, I helped my teams win, and winning is everything in prison. Nobody remembers who came in second. Winning, like possessing information, is also power.

As for being challenged, my reputation for not backing down helped to keep me out of fights. I remember one occasion when a clique of four guys was walking the tiers. The joint, as I've mentioned, was wide open back then, and you could go wherever you wanted. Just pay the goons and you had free passage.

In any event, I knew one of the four guys in the aforementioned clique, and I asked him what they were doing. He said, "We're looking for rapo's to kill."

I got my jacket on and put my sign out for the guard to hit my cell door. My acquaintance asked me what I was doing and I told him I was coming out to deal with it. My acquaintance said no, they weren't talking about me.

Each time I was challenged, I would challenge the person back. This kept me out of fights, as I say, but during all this time I didn't develop much in the way of victim empathy, anger management, or impulse control because I never talked about rape and I never talked about myself. I was finally released in 1986. Five months later I was back in prison because I had re-offended.

This time I was sent to the Twin Rivers Correctional Facility (TRCC). It was a few hundred yards from WSR and I could see the outside of the big wall. TRCC was new and clean. The state was instituting a sex offender treatment program there. I took part in some of it, but kept as low a profile as I could. The less people knew about me, the better.

After a few years, I told the treatment staff that I was going to try to get minimum custody so that I could go to the Honor Farm. The treatment staff told me that I would have to give up that idea and stay with the treatment program. I said no. They didn't like an inmate telling them "no" so they arranged for my transfer to "The Walls" (Washington State Penitentiary at Walla Walla). I was only there about a year, but it seemed like forever. Walla Walla was uglier and dirtier than WSR. It was older and more violent.

Since I had been in the system for so many years, my crime was known when I got to The Walls. I had been inside The Walls for several months, and was just getting ready for a transfer to the medium security section, when I was challenged once again. But in this one particular instance, I chose not to answer the challenge. To do so would have jeopardized my transfer to the medium security wing, and I was not about to do that.

The incident began when a couple of guys came into my cell and said I had to get out. A lot of the other guys on the block were yelling and calling me rapo. The guards heard the clamor, so I went to them and said I was having a problem. The sergeant said what normally happens is that I would get in a fight and then I would be taken to the hole for disciplinary reasons. I said I had no intention of getting into a fight because I was scheduled for a transfer the next morning. The sergeant looked disappointed. The poor guy wouldn't get his kicks.

I was transferred to the medium wing the next morning, but one of the guys who had come into my cell was transferred at the same time. Consequently, within a few days, my crime, once again, was well known.

Fortunately for me, my athletic abilities were also well known in medium security. I was recruited to play on a softball team within an hour of my arrival. But then one of the guys on the team wanted to talk to me, so I went out to the yard. The guy came up to me and said, "I ain't playing on no team with no rapo." I told him I understood how he felt but I would not quit the team. If they wanted me off, they would all have to tell me. They took a vote and I was kicked off the team. I joined another team and we won first place that year, so in retrospect it was a good move.

During my first week in medium, I was getting ready to take a shower and this guy came in and asked if I was in for rape. I said yes I was and started to put my pants back on for whatever trouble was about to come my way.

The guy turned around and went back to wherever he'd come from, but a few minutes later he returned. He asked me how old the woman was. I said I didn't know her exact age. He then asked me if the woman had been black and I said, "No."

"Too bad," he said, and left.

Interlude

Vengeance

by Robert Ellis Gordon

Do I contradict myself?
                Very well then, I contradict myself
(I am large and contain multitudes)

                Walt Whitman, *Leaves of Grass*

No prison has managed to gnaw away at my soul like the Twin Rivers Correctional Center. TRCC is one of those three, high security prisons that sit atop the big hill overlooking the town of Monroe, and it's the one I cut my teeth on back in 1989. I taught frequently at Twin Rivers until December 1992. Then the chill of administrative disapproval descended, and I have not been invited back since.

You can be sure that I felt the chill. But I never heard specifics, just rumors. According to the rumors, the administration had come to view me with loathing and contempt. I was a trouble maker, I heard, a loose cannon, a liberal, and, worst of all, I was suffering from the syndrome known as "drift."

"Drift" is not only a lovely sounding term, but a deceptively powerful concept; one of those poetic eruptions that occur with surprising frequency on the metamorphic continent of prison jargon. What it means is that I identified too closely with my students—that I was not maintaining a professional distance—and, truth to tell, if I'd ever been confronted by the charge, I would've been hard-pressed to deny it. You see, the more time I spend with court-certified villains, the more time I spend in prison classrooms, the less difference I see between myself and my students, and between me and them and all of you outside.

But be that as it may, the rumors didn't ruin my career. I've taught at five prisons and four juvenile detention facilities since I was banished from Twin Rivers. Still, the dread hasn't faded with the passage of time: when I think about Twin Rivers, I recoil.

Constructed in 1982, Twin Rivers is a modern affair that does not exist on the same architectural planet as the original McNeil Island or, for that matter, as the Washington State Reformatory, which is located a stone's throw away on the other side of that hill.

The Reformatory, as Duane Eaglestaff points out, is a classic Cagney/Bogart joint, a turn of the century steel, brick, and concrete fortress replete with barred cells, a massive bull yard, and a ceaseless cacophony of shouts, curses, and eerie tunnel-magnified echoes. At twenty-seven feet, the Reformatory's walls are the highest in the state corrections system, and the color of the place is as institutional a brown as the fields outside are verdant green. Speaking strictly from the standpoint of aesthetics, in short, the Reformatory is a prison that reeks of prison, and, over time, I have come to appreciate its honesty in that regard.

The same cannot be said of Twin Rivers. To be sure, TRCC's perimeter is skirted by many large rolls of barbed razor wire, and beyond the razor wire there is the obligatory metal detector, the occasional pat search, and the ritual dabbing of the hand with invisible ink which shows up as a pleasing neon-tetra blue when passed under a special light; which **must** show up when passed under that light if a male visitor wishes to leave the prison in an expeditious manner. The dabbing is followed by a stop and go walk through three sets of electronically controlled doors, no more than one of which may be unlocked at any given time.

These routine security matters aside, however, once you're inside of Twin Rivers, there's no Cagney/Bogart bull yard, for starters. Instead, there's a lawn, a velvety close-cropped golf course type of lawn that only those inmates who want to risk an infraction would presume to tread upon. There aren't any signs that tell you to keep off the grass, nor is there a need for such signs. One look around; one deep slow breath, one true hit of the local ambiance is enough to let you know that here at Twin Rivers we stay on the sidewalks, we don't skip or run, and we always keep our hands to ourselves.

The south side of the compound is a concrete long house, a one-story series of administrative offices and classrooms, a barber shop, a print shop, and a gym. But it is the four living units (not "cell blocks," please) that make Twin Rivers so strikingly unsuitable for use as a prison movie set. These three-story buildings do not contain barred cells: instead they contain dorm rooms. They are not painted institutional brown but rather cobalt blue. They have practical names—A-Unit, B-Unit, C-Unit, and D-Unit—and their box-next-to-box-upon-box design makes them the Mother of all Lego projects.

Twin Rivers reeks of bland symmetry, in short, of every sterile complex (condo/retirement/you-name-it) ever constructed. But appearances can be deceiving, and TRCC's outward sterility notwithstanding, there was something unmanageable at work there, some insidious madness that could not be concealed by any amount of marching in file beside an immaculate lawn; that refused to be smothered by tons of concrete, even though the concrete was painted a friendly blue.

I felt it the first day I walked into Twin Rivers, and it was never something I got used to. On the contrary, fear crept up on me over the years until it reached the point where I never felt emotionally safe in that place, at least not until the classroom door closed and I was finally alone with my students. And even then, I admit, I frequently wondered how many student snitches I had in class, and how many listening devices and video cameras were planted in the walls.

Paranoia, you say? I agree. The stuff was oozing out of me. And it was oozing out of my students. And all the staff members I knew were riddled with pathology, especially the ones who never acknowledged the stress; who never owned up to the heavy toll exacted by the thoroughly twisted nature of their workplace. Obviously, the cool professional demeanor with which they comported themselves represented nothing more than feigned self-possession, and, just as obviously, this *proved* they were in denial.

Unless, of course, I was wrong. Unless, of course I was projecting. ("Denial" and "projection" are words, by the way, that they wouldn't have much use for at the old-fashioned joint next door, but which, along with many other pop-psych terms, are very much in vogue at Twin Rivers.)

You see, Twin Rivers is not just any prison. Twin Rivers is a specialty prison. Although it houses a few garden variety criminals—drug dealers, robbers, murderers, and the lot—it is primarily in the sex offense business. Or, to be more precise, Twin Rivers is in the business of overhauling the souls of those rapists, child molesters, perpetrators of incest, and other sexual deviants who have volunteered to enter the Sex Offender Treatment Program (SOTP) and who have been deemed amenable to treatment.

In the spring of 1998, there were 175 participants in SOTP. In addition, 201 inmates at Twin Rivers were marking time while waiting for an opening in the program, and another 1,632 sex offenders currently residing at other prisons in the state had put in for transfers to the institution that is commonly referred to as "Pervert U" by many of Washington's 12,000-plus convicts (any number of whom are, themselves, convicted sex offenders who are, for reasons of survival and/or the need to fabricate a sense of self-esteem, attempting to pass themselves off as drug dealers, burglars, or, for the truly bold liars, as bank robbers and fearless killers).

In the past, it was *de rigeur* for any sex offender to try to keep the nature of his crime to himself because, as you know, snitches and sex offenders share the bottom of the brutal prison pecking order. The threat of exposure, in fact, was sometimes used by staff to turn sex offenders into snitches. What comes as news then, is that so many rapists and child molesters have openly declared themselves by volunteering to enter an experimental program that began in 1988 with only twenty-two participants. This sudden rush to join up may reflect a sincere desire on the part of these men to change. Or it may reflect an equally sincere, indeed desperate desire to *appear* to have changed, owing to the massive hammer that the State of Washington is holding over the heads of its convicted sex offenders.

The name of this hammer is the Civil Commitment Act. As noted earlier, it was passed in the spring of 1990, a year after a developmentally disabled man named Earl Shriner, who had a long history of sexual assaults against children, raped a six-year-old boy in a park in Tacoma, ripped the boy's penis off, and left him in a pile of leaves to die. The boy did not die; Shriner was apprehended within days, and public outrage was vast and enduring. The story played on the news for months.

At the governor's behest a task force on sex crimes was formed, and a number of its recommendations became law. These laws led to longer sentences; mandatory registration of sex offenders who are released into the community; and the concomitant posting, at the discretion of local law enforcement officials, of bulletins, replete with a mug shot, that announce the arrival of a high-risk sexual predator and provide the ex-convict's address. As you might expect, more than one recently released sex offender has been run out of town, and in the summer 1993, some residents of a neighborhood in Lynnwood, Washington, torched the house of a soon-to-be released child molester.

Still, the most controversial of the new laws was the Civil Commitment Act. The Act provides prosecutors with the option of retrying a sex offender after he has completed his prison sentence, to determine if he is likely to strike again. If the jury rules against the defendant (and thus far, every jury has) the sex offender is sent to a Land of No Return called the Special Commitment Center (SCC). While there are plans afoot to move the SCC to the newly constructed McNeil Island Corrections Center, the SCC is presently located in a wing of the third prison that sits atop the hill overlooking Monroe. The name of that prison is the Special Offender Center (SOC).

Constructed, like Twin Rivers, in 1982, the SOC is a dreadful and dominating presence. Originally intended to house Washington's criminally insane, the SOC dwarfs the Reformatory and Twin Rivers in both physical scale and punitive mission. Its residents live in a state of near total lockdown and, as evidence of the misery they endure, some of those who've been civilly committed have sued not for freedom but for the right to return to a conventional prison.

I am told there are a few windows in the SOC; a sufficient number, at any rate, to enable the residents to differentiate between night and day, and that this, in turn, helps to keep the ones who aren't already insane from going insane. If these windows really do exist, they must be exceptionally narrow and deeply recessed because they are simply not visible from a hundred yards off. When gazing at the SOC the word "forbidding" comes to mind, but it doesn't begin to do the edifice justice, and I don't know of any word that does. Even veteran, prison-hardened staff members tend to avert their eyes when the SOC comes into view.

Upon commitment to the SCC, a sex offender's status changes from "convict" to "patient," and neither his new status nor his new address will change unless and until a sentence review board determines that he has been cured of deviant urges. To date, no civilly committed patient has been deemed cured, and no one, least of all the patients, ever expects it to happen. Even the judges who have ruled the Act constitutional have twice scolded the state with regard to this matter of cure. The first scolding occurred when it was revealed, a couple of years following the law's enactment, that no treatment was being offered. Shortly thereafter the state was scolded again for offering treatment that was conducted by thoroughly unqualified personnel.

Opponents have argued, unsuccessfully, that the Civil Commitment Act is an illegal end run around the rules of evidence, based as it is on crimes that have never been committed. Proponents have argued, curiously enough, not that their prognostications are perfectly accurate, but that they can divine the commission of a future sex crime with an accuracy rate of 33 percent. One can only speculate as to how they came up with the number 33, as opposed, say, to 29 or 47.

Questions of statistical and constitutional niceties aside, however, there is no doubt but that the Civil Commitment Act gets the job done. It puts our sex fiends away, far far away, presumably for the rest of their lives. For traumatized victims and for potential future victims, the Act is the next best thing to pre-emptive capital punishment. And for the sex offenders, themselves, the Act functions in much the same way. Simply serving out a prison sentence may no longer be the harshest price they pay. In fact, prison time may turn out to be the mildest punishment a sex offender receives. Civil Commitment is a mighty hammer indeed.

Thus the sudden rush to sign up for Twin Rivers' Sex Offender Treatment Program. But this rush must not be mistaken for a statistically significant rate of cure. To begin with, not all 3,000-plus sex offenders who are currently incarcerated in the State of Washington have applied for admission to the SOTP, and not all who've applied have been deemed amenable to treatment. Moreover, of those who've been accepted to the program, between 60 and 70 percent have either quit or been asked to leave within six months of their matriculation. Ultimately, then, only a very small number of the state's convicted sex offenders—a mere 740 over the past decade—have made it through the entire treatment program.

The men who do complete the SOTP take part in a wide range of activities designed to soften if not break their deviant urges, to provide them with the tools necessary to recognize the onset of deviant behavior, and, it is hoped, to arrest the process before they commit another act of sexual violence. Among the more routine staples of the SOTP are stress and anger management classes; sex education classes; group therapy; assertiveness training; victim empathy training; drug and alcohol counseling; and relapse prevention training.

Among the more unusual methodologies employed in the treatment of sex offenders are counter-conditioning activities designed to alter an offender's pattern of sexual arousal. Most of these activities involve some combination of the following: verbalization of deviant sexual fantasies; contemporaneous masturbation; contemporaneous visualization of something the offender finds disgusting (e.g. a toilet bowl full of feces), and/or the introduction of a nausea inducing gas just prior to the offender's climax.

While there is nothing comical about the aforementioned techniques—or about the behaviors that elicited their inventions—there is at least something incongruous about their titles. Not many of us would, upon hearing the terms "minimal arousal conditioning," "olfactory aversion therapy," or "assisted covert desensitization," picture a man in a room shouting deviant fantasies into a tape recorder while he is furiously jerking off. But that is what transpires. And, in the realm of the therapeutically bizarre, that isn't all that transpires. In addition, SOTP participants are hooked up, on a regular basis, to a technologically advanced—if appalling—machine called a penile plethysmograph.

A plethysmograph (the Greek root for which is *pleth*, an enlargement) is defined, by Webster's, as "an instrument for determining the variations in the size of an organ or a limb." According to the U.S.

Justice Department's publication, *A Practitioner's Guide to Treating the Incarcerated Male Sex Offender*, plethysmography works like this:

> An electronic device, called a penile transducer, is attached to the penis by the client. It detects changes in the size of an organ from a state of no sexual arousal (flaccidity) to a state of complete arousal (full erection). If one presents stimuli of both deviant and non-deviant content to a client while measuring his sexual response, the associated degrees of erection provide an indication of his sexual interests, preferences, and inhibitions.

The stimuli presented are slides or photographs of a prurient nature—dirty pictures, if you will—that vary according to gender and, as a *Seattle Times* reporter once delicately phrased it, "differing levels of consent." A no-nonsense counselor over at the Reformatory put it somewhat less delicately to me: "Animals, naked kids, blood, the works. The sky's the limit with that thing."

The plethysmograph has proven useful for diagnosing a sex offender's particular brand of deviance; for fine-tuning a customized program designed to bring about a diminishment in the offender's deviant urges; and for monitoring the offender's progress (or lack thereof) as he proceeds through the SOTP. In the aforementioned *Practitioner's Guide*, under the subheading "Minimization of Client Misrepresentation," it is noted that:

> Sex offenders are notorious for misrepresenting their favorite fantasies and behaviors....Since the plethysmograph does not rely entirely on the honesty of self-report...the assessment procedure may yield information that the offender has been reluctant to disclose. The penile plethysmograph represents the only objective, valid method of assessing an offender's sexual arousal pattern.

Or, as Nobel Laureate Isaac Bashevis Singer stated more succinctly, "The penis never lies."

Of course that doesn't mean that the man the penis is attached to isn't capable of lying to win his freedom, or that the penis, itself, won't have a change of heart, so to speak, if it ever gets back on the streets. I was reminded of this one wet December evening in 1991 as I was leaving Twin Rivers after class. My escort on that occasion was a gentle and usually circumspect member of the recreation staff. On this night, however, he nodded toward the many inmates who were marching from their living units to the chow hall and let me in on his thoughts. "Most of those guys," he said, "are just assholes."

I respected that observation, I really did. It was precisely the sort of statement we don't get enough of these days, the type that cuts through layer upon arcane layer of academic/bureaucratic/psychobabble bullshit, and gets to the heart of the matter. They are predators first and foremost, my friend seemed to be saying. And so what if they're not in Ted Bundy's league? They're dependable fellows, the utility infielders of incest, rape, and child molestation, who can be counted upon, whenever given the chance, to go out and get the job done.

My friend, a career corrections man, had spoken with the authority of one who knows. Granted, there are exceptions; granted, there are one-time perpetrators. But sex offenders are not only notorious liars, they are notorious recidivists as well. So where, in the end, do we come down on these fellows, on these home-grown fathers, brothers, and sons who have committed unspeakable crimes? Do we hate them because of the evil they've done and are statistically liable to do again? Or do we love the sinner and hate the sin as Jesus recommended?

I don't have the answers to those questions: I just live with the contradictions. You see, inside the prison classroom—even at Twin Rivers—I was fiercely devoted to my students. I was so devoted, in fact, so immersed in their work; so utterly consumed by and drunk on their words, on their oft-searing autobiographical stories, and on their sorry and luckless and so completely fucked up that they verged on the beautiful lives...well, I tended to forget that I was dealing with men who had raped and molested children. I came to view them as normal human beings.

But what happens when I'm outside of prison? How do I regard those men then? Let me relate a minor anecdote. It's about a crime that never happened. I was ten years old when the crime didn't happen, and I lived in suburban Boston. One day, for a reason I can't remember, I rode the subway downtown. Perhaps I was visiting my dad at his office. Perhaps there was a new exhibit at the science museum. I just can't remember why I went. But I do remember this: when I walked underground to catch the subway home, I was approached by a man who, I now realize, was a child molester. He helped me onto the streetcar by placing his hand on my ass and pushing me through the crowded doorway. Then he took me by the arm and guided me to an empty double seat in the back. He sat down next to me. He was wearing white painter's overalls.

The man, whose face I can't recall, started talking in a hyper nonstop fashion. I did my best to ignore him and stared out the window at the passing tunnel walls. I was doing a pretty fair job of shutting out his voice until he mentioned "messing around." He asked me if I'd ever "messed around." I had no idea what he meant, but the wise child in me sensed danger. So without a word I got up from my seat and left the streetcar at the next stop. Fortunately, the man didn't follow.

Thus, as noted, no crime was committed, and the foiled attempt occurred more than thirty years ago. Nevertheless, if I were to meet the man in the white overalls today, I'd want an opportunity to get back at him. I'd be most appreciative, in fact, if the state arranged a closed-door session for just the two of us. Just he and I alone in a room. I think it's a swell idea. He'd be handcuffed, of course, and his feet would be shackled, whereas I'd be free to roam about as I pleased. I'd throw a punch now and then, in a leisurely fashion, whenever the spirit moved me. I imagine that a few swift kicks to his balls would also prove to be gratifying. It's a fitting scenario, don't you agree? The only flaw in the plan—the only obstacle I foresee—is my potential inability to fully exploit it, to hold up my end of the rigged fight. He'd be an old man by now, after all. And old or young the smell of blood isn't pleasant, nor is the sight of broken flesh and splintered teeth.

It's a problem, alright, the hands-on aspect. I'll just have to harden my resolve when the time arrives. In the interim, however, it's important to note that my encounter with the man in the white overalls was not the stuff of major trauma, not even close. I hardly ever think about the incident. But I do have a vengeful streak. When I read about those trappers up in Alaska who torture wolves with their cruel, metal snares; when I see a parent hit a toddler in the supermarket; or whenever I see anyone beating a dog...well it makes me a little crazy. I feel this palpable wrath, this tempest inside, and it instructs me to lash out with my fists. But since the state won't allow that, and since I fear the state, I know my desires are relatively harmless, that my vengeful inclinations won't be realized. And that's certainly a blessing for me and the state: it keeps my violence in check.

Still, I really wouldn't mind it, I wouldn't mind it a bit, if there was a state-sanctioned alternative for my impulses; some mechanism by which the state vented my rage, albeit in a manner that was constitutionally acceptable; that was more genteel, so to speak, than my crude musings. And in one arena I know of, my wish is granted. In fact it's granted in spades every day.

To wit: if we revisit the man in the white overalls—that sick son of a bitch who did me no harm but surely had evil intent—well he just might get caught someday. And what if, as a consequence, he is sent to Twin Rivers, a prison that in mission and design, George Orwell himself could not improve upon? And what if Big Brother lives in that prison, and I don't mean metaphorically, I mean He *lives* there. And what if, in His right hand, He holds a crackerjack squad of plethysmograph-wielding Thought Police? And what if, in His left hand, Big Brother holds an edifice, a vast edifice called the Special Offender Center? And what if any convict who is sent to that edifice never returns again?

And what if by lying—by not owning up—to every deviant act in his repertoire: what if, in other words, by trying to fool the unfoolable Thought Police—the man in the overalls merely sets himself up for designation as an untreatable sexual predator, and hence commitment to the SCC? And what if (just to make his plight deliciously worse), telling the truth won't help? What if (this happens) by revealing it all; by leaving no morsel, no unreported crime, no unacted-upon fantasy unconfessed—he simply turns himself into a prosecutor's dream, an ideal candidate for Civil Commitment? What if, in short, the state sets a trap from which the man in the white overalls can't escape?

This is my answer: applause. I, who am fiercely devoted to my students, I who love them, bask in them, and do my best to tell the world that they are utterly human and redeemable . . . well I'd change my tune when it came to the man who tried to fondle, rape, and/or kill me. I'd ask the state to show him no mercy. And if the state succeeded in banishing the man to The Edifice of No Return, I'd shake the state's hand for a job well done. I'd say, "Thank you for crushing the bastard."

4 | Something Holy

Keith R. Landsdowne is representative of a remarkable sub-strata of the prison culture. This sub-strata is composed of men who have hit a bottom so low that you and I would never want to catch even the faintest vicarious whiff of it. They've endured the worst punishments that the system metes out, sometimes for years at a stretch. And they've managed, God knows how, to survive.

What they've gone through has made these men as tough as tempered steel, though I've never met one who exuded bitterness. On the contrary. Those convicts who've ascended from Jailhouse Hell tend to emanate an other-worldly radiance.

Whenever I encounter a survivor like Keith, I know I'm in the presence of something holy.

Choosing Sanity

by Keith R. Lansdowne

I N 1984, I WAS TWENTY-FOUR YEARS OLD and six years into a twenty-year sentence for the crime of Murder in the Second Degree. I was incarcerated at the Washington State Penitentiary at Walla Walla. At that time, Walla Walla was reputed to be one of the most violent and dangerous prisons in the country.

Back then I had been doing fairly well by prison standards. I hadn't been charged with any major rule violation for a while, and I was working in the prison metal plant, pressing license plates and earning up to $1.00 per hour. We still had a higher education program in those days, and I was thinking of pursuing an AA degree in Business Administration.

Out in the Big Yard tension was high, and many people, myself included, routinely carried shanks (homemade knives) because no one knew just when things would explode. Lots of fights were taking place, and no one was comfortable. A major riot could occur at any time.

During the course of a routine shakedown by the guards, my shank was discovered. As a consequence, I was sent to the Intensive Management Unit (IMU), which is a fancy-sounding title for solitary confinement, otherwise known as "the hole."

Prison policy dictated that any convict entering the IMU be subjected to a body cavity search, which is to say a digital rectal probe. Or, to put it in street vernacular, anyone going to the IMU was subject to having a finger shoved up his ass.

Naturally, I objected to this policy. As a result, when the guards came to transport me to IMU, they came in force. Five guards physically overwhelmed me, while one guard videotaped the anal assault. Following the digital rape, I was taken to the IMU and placed in a cell.

The cell was nine feet long and five feet wide. It had a six-inch wide slit of a window, along with two florescent lights, one of which remained on twenty-four hours a day. I was confined to this tiny cell with the eternal fluorescent light for twenty-three hours and fifty minutes of every day. During the remaining ten minutes, I was permitted to take a shower.

The day after my arrival in IMU, I was served with a notice that I was being charged with violation of a major rule. Specifically, I was charged with assault on a staff member. This arose from my refusal to submit to anal rape peacefully.

I had been jumped by five men, forcibly subjected to having a finger shoved up my ass, chained up, dragged, thrown, tossed, and finally beaten. And for this I was charged with assault!

At the hearing for this rule violation I was, of course, found guilty. As a sanction, my stay in isolation was extended.

While I was in IMU, I was required to submit to a strip search prior to leaving my cell for any reason. This was degrading. And the act of dressing and undressing gave the guards numerous opportunities to make fun of my pink-tinged IMU overalls, to tell me how alluring I looked. The guards rarely missed an opportunity to taunt me or any other IMU resident. It didn't require much courage on their part: whenever we left our cells, we were handcuffed with our hands behind our backs. In addition, we were escorted by a minimum of two guards, and sometimes by more than two.

I must admit, even in the face of the guards' superior numbers, not to mention the shackles I wore and the threat of further sanctions, I allowed myself to be goaded by the taunting; I succumbed to the rage that it triggered. On too many occasions I tried my best to cause one or more of the guards enough pain to think twice before tormenting me again. Every time I did this, I lost. Every time I did this, I was beaten. And every time I wound up with yet more sanctions, more time in IMU.

After ten months in IMU, I was released. This came as a surprise to me because I'd given up on my efforts to keep track of time; given up on my efforts to know how many more days would pass before I'd get to leave "the hole." When I rejoined the general prison population I felt very lucky, like a man who'd just won the lottery.

Unfortunately, it was a short-lived victory. Exactly one week after my release, I was returned to IMU. I was sent back because, unbeknownst to me, one of my three new cellmates had jerry-rigged an extension cord in order to heat water for instant coffee. And this extension cord was (I'm not kidding here) deemed by the authorities to be an explosive device, which is to say a home-made bomb! To make matters worse, prison policy stated that "Any person in a multiple man cell shall be deemed guilty of anything said/done/or found in that cell, unless he/she can prove otherwise."

In addition to being sent back to IMU, I lost 540 days of "good time." Thus, my cellmate's jerry-rigged extension cord was very costly indeed: it meant that I'd be spending an extra year and a half in prison.

As I faced the prospect of IMU again, I heard an audible click in the back of my mind. It is embarrassing and even painful to admit my train of thought. It was, "Eighteen months of good time lost because of an extension cord? Back to IMU and another round with the rapo squad? They want to play hardball? Okay, but this time, I play, too. If I'm going to lose a year and a half, I'm going to earn it!"

Not a very rational way to think, was it? And I was not a very rational man. For many, many months—for more than two years, in fact—rage was the only emotion I knew. I fought the guards, though I was shackled and outnumbered. I taunted, abused, and vilified them, knowing full well it would result in beatings and further sanctions. I threw food, water, urine, and excrement on the guards. I went weeks without eating or talking to any staff. It was the darkest, loneliest time I have ever known. Even now it is terrifying to remember those months I spent in the abyss, and how close I came to never returning.

If you were one with whom I corresponded during this period, I doubt you comprehended how far I'd strayed over the edge. For the only moments of sanity I knew were the moments I spent writing or receiving letters. Fortunately, I was blessed by people who encouraged me to keep my pen in hand, to keep corresponding no matter what. To those faithful friends I owe a debt of gratitude that no amount of riches could ever repay. My friends provided me with a handhold on reality, albeit a tenuous one.

Looking back on that time, one moment in particular stands out. I remember it as if it occurred yesterday. I can still hear a voice in my mind saying, "What the hell are you doing?" I was sitting on the floor of my cell rubbing my thigh after having just endured a sound beating by four guards. They'd jumped me because, after having left me for an hour in the locked shower stall, I'd made reference to their mongrel dog ancestors.

I rubbed my thigh and gasped for air. Something told me, as I sat there, that this was the moment when I could choose to continue my descent into insanity or climb back up to the realm of reality.

I realized the latter would require a vast amount of work. To achieve a state of sanity I would have to figure out who I was, where I was, where I came from, and where I wanted to go. I would have to turn inward, to face my rage, to understand it, to deal with it, and, ultimately, to let it go.

That task was far more formidable and terrifying than was my entry into prison so many years before. Some small voice told me that the task would be more difficult than anything I'd ever undertaken, and that, therefore, I must follow that path.

So alone and afraid, I set out. This journey took me deeply into myself, and that is one place most human beings never want to go. Initially, it reduced me to a man with no pride, no sense of self-worth, and no false illusions. But ultimately, once I'd hit bottom, I acquired the freedom to accept the gifts that life brought my way.

Once I embarked on my way back to sanity, it took a mere seven months to gain release from IMU. But my ascent wasn't and still isn't complete. I've come to know it's a journey that's never completed. Each day brings new revelations, and I rejoice in the opportunity to experience them.

Today, as I near the end of my twenty-year prison sentence, I consider myself to be a lucky man. I have friends who helped me to regain a place in the human community. Yet I am aware that I left many men back in IMU, men who were not as fortunate as I. They are utterly alone and living in Hell. That is important to remember.

Interlude

Multiculturalism

by Robert Ellis Gordon

One of the last prison classes I taught included, among others, a black nationalist, a white supremacist, a traditional Eskimo, some born again Christians, an assortment of nihilists, and one Jew. Outside of class, my supervisor informed me, most of these guys couldn't talk to each other. But in order to make the workshop function, the students were required to hang their swaggers at the door, and to treat each other and each other's work with respect.

The makeup of the class was not atypical for a prison workshop. Nor, as I thought the matter over, was the makeup of the class dissimilar to that of many work crews I'd been a part of on numerous blue collar jobs.

This has led me to conclude that when my university counterparts sit around and pat one another on the back for bringing "diversity" to their departments, they aren't talking about genuine diversity. Rather, they're talking about diversity that is contrived, about diversity that is imposed by upper class professionals who have the option of *not* working or living with "those people" they are so proud of sharing office space with.

Real diversity isn't contrived, nor is it a matter of choice. Authentic multicultural interaction, in my experience, takes place when convicted felons or the working poor are thrown together and forced to co-exist by people in authority who, as a general rule, don't give a shit about them.

5 | Childhood

From 1991 through 1995, I taught frequently at the Washington State Reformatory in Monroe. One of my students was Michael Collins. Collins, you may recall, was serving a stretch for committing a string of armed robberies.

His stories, as evidenced by the one that follows, are palpably brutal and bleak. Some of my friends, who have never been incarcerated, find his stories to be too bleak. But in the context of prison, Collins's stories aren't shocking or unique. Far from it. As I bounced from prison to prison throughout the 1990s, encouraging my students to mine their pasts, to dip into their childhoods to find their true stories, I encountered myriad variations on Collins's themes. Though the particulars differed from author to author, all the stories boiled down to one story. It's the story of children who are faced with bad choices (a bad choice being the absence of good choices). It's the story of children raising themselves in a world, like the prisons they grew up to inhabit, that offers precious few options and little hope.

The Shoe Box

a story by Michael Collins

SCOTTY DIDN'T MIND so much that his mom's boyfriend, Steve, pissed all over Scotty's bedroom floor. Scotty never slept there. He usually passed out on the couch after watching the movie on "Action Theater" or "Portland Wrestling" or "The Joan Rivers Show." It had been Buddy Rose who slapped some unknown wrestler on the chest at about the same time Steve staggered out of a drunken sleep into the hallway. In a pair of baggy Fruit of the Loom briefs he stood scratching his crotch with one hand, his beard with the other, taking tiny steps in place to keep his balance. Steve looked through the door on the left, the bathroom, and then walked through the door on the right. Scotty didn't have to hear the sound of someone pissing to know what was happening. He didn't try to stop him.

Scotty's room was colder than the rest of the house, and while it didn't smell of urine as Scotty thought it should, he wondered why his dog, Samantha, had chosen this room to have her puppies. Everything in the room was hard: his dresser, his Little League trophies, his fishing poles and tackle boxes, his outdated Murray bicycle. Even the carpet was stiff and unyielding.

Six of the eight puppies had died two days before, and Scotty thought four of those were stillborn since the other two were warm when he found them. He had placed each of the dead puppies softly inside a plastic garbage bag and tied it off as tightly as he could. His mom was glad the puppies died, he knew. She couldn't afford to feed one hundred and fucking one Dalmatians, she'd said. Scotty buried the bag in the woods behind Old Man Sawyer's trailer. It was the only place he could walk to with a shovel and a bag full of dead puppies without being seen.

He slid a bowl of water under the bed. Samantha, a solid brown cocker spaniel, lifted her head and looked at Scotty through the darkness. She lay her head back down and breathed a loud sigh. The puppies lay sprawled out on the carpet in front of her, whimpering, blindly turning their heads this way and that. Scotty reached under and picked up one of the puppies and sat it next to Samantha. He started to pick up the other one when he heard a low, snarling growl. He pulled his arm out from under the bed and watched as Samantha pushed the puppy away from her with her snout. The puppy whimpered loudly and Samantha looked at Scotty with fearful eyes like she'd done something wrong. Scotty touched the puppy farthest from Samantha. She just looked at him, breathing. He picked the puppy up. She looked at Scotty still, her eyes glossy. He held the puppy out in front of Samantha. She growled.

Scotty set the puppy down a couple of feet from Samantha and went to get some milk. His mother stood in the doorway, just awake, pushing the hair out of her face like someone peering through a set of drapes.

"They're gonna' die, honey" she said.

"I can feed them," Scotty said.

"Yeah, well by the time you get home from basketball practice they'll be pretty hungry."

Scotty said nothing.

"They kept me up all morning, Scotty. Damnit," she said, "I can't work if I can't sleep."

Scotty wanted to suggest that Steve could feed the puppies in the morning. He wanted to say the fat fucker did nothing but sit on his ass all day so why couldn't he feed the puppies? But he knew better. Steve wasn't going to do shit, and Scotty didn't like the idea of Steve messing with his dog, anyway. Come to think of it, Scotty didn't like Steve sitting on the couch or watching the TV either.

"Maybe I can give them to someone," Scotty said.

"You don't give someone puppies that might die," she said.

Scotty knew she was right. He also knew the puppies were suffering, that they were going to die just like the others. But he wasn't going to make it easy for his mom. He was going to make her tell him to do it.

"If you want I can drive you out to Circle Bridge on my way to work," she said.

Scotty thought of cleaning fish and finding puppy bones in the belly of a catfish, of dead puppies splashing and whining and looking at him through phosphorescent eyes every time he walked by there at night on his way home from the Garzas' place.

"No," he said.

"They're going to *die*, Scott. And I'm not going to sit and listen to them while they do. So you can either put them in the wood shed and let them die out there, or you can put them out of their misery. I don't want them in the house when I get home."

She walked across the hall into the bathroom and slammed the door. Scotty wondered why she didn't just piss on the floor like everyone else.

Scotty grabbed a Nike shoe box from his shelf and emptied its contents onto his bed. Among the letters from his cousins in Ohio and baseball cards and parts from a dismantled walkie-talkie lay an old picture of his dad leaning against his truck with beer in hand, smiling. Scotty wondered how his dad would kill the puppies. He swept up the letters and pictures and pieces of plastic and put them in a drawer. He lined the bottom of the shoe box with an old T-shirt and then placed the puppies inside, closing them in with the orange and white lid. He heard muffled whining coming from the box.

He put the box down and knelt next to the bed, not caring if he was kneeling in Steve's dried piss. He told Samantha he was sorry all her puppies had to die, noticing at once how his voice didn't sound like his own. The toilet flushed across the hall and Scotty quickly got to his feet and took the shoe box out to the wood shed.

In the corner of the wood shed was a pile of hoes and shovels and axes. The walls were adorned with hand-held scythes and hoses, all suitable instruments for killing little puppies. He could even use one of the nails that held a bunch of fan belts. For that matter, he could use the red, five-gallon gas can, or the two-stroke mix inside, or the gas-powered weed eater. He could probably use everything from the sawdust and slivers and dirt on the floor to the very walls of the wood shed. Killing puppies would be simple when you thought about it.

Scotty sat on the chopping block. He opened the shoe box and set it on his lap. The two puppies leaned against one another in what appeared to be an attempt at keeping warm, but Scotty didn't see how it worked. Trying to stand on weak legs, the two puppies only bumped head to rump or head to head, falling back, crawling in circles around each other. He wished they were sleeping.

Scotty set the shoe box on the floor and replaced the lid. He stood and looked around. He walked outside and stopped to look at the house. He thought of Steve sitting on the couch, laughing at the TV, farting on the cushions that covered only half the crack of his ass. He went back inside the wood shed and took a broken axe handle from the pile in the corner. He pulled one puppy from the shoe box and set it on the chopping block. It whimpered, its head lifted, tilted as if listening for something. Scotty brought the axe handle down hard on its neck. The puppy was dead. A trickle of blood seeped up from its nose and mouth onto the chopping block. Scotty picked it up. It was warm and soft and loose. The Woodford's Doberman was the father. Scotty could see the resemblance now; narrow jaw, pointy ears. He turned it over and looked between its legs. It was a girl. Scotty put the axe handle on the ground. He picked up the other puppy and put the dead one back in the shoe box. He picked up the axe handle, set the puppy on the maple chopping block, and hit it hard on the head. This time the puppy's hind legs convulsed and quivered, its head pinned to the chopping block. Scotty hit it again, smashing its skull and finishing it. There was blood on the axe handle, more on the chopping block, with bits of hair.

He put the second puppy in the shoe box next to the first and then put the shoe box inside a plastic garbage bag and tied it off. He buried the two puppies next to where he had buried the others, along with the axe handle, and then walked home.

Interlude

The Lie

by Robert Ellis Gordon

Prisons are hard places to get into and harder yet to get out of. There are not many of us for whom the membrane is permeable, and darting in and out of institutions as I do affords me a luxury that no convict I've ever met can boast of: a modicum of non-attachment.

Still, even sporadic immersion in the prison environment can exact a price on the soul, and the price may manifest itself in unusual ways. Take, for example, the phenomenon of staring with unseeing eyes. I do not mean this in the hyperbolic sense of the term, as a figure of speech that implies that the one who is staring sees something but not everything in his field of vision. What I mean is more precise, more literal than that, and it went on for almost two years. It is worth noting, perhaps, that the prison writing workshops I lead, which average about eighteen students, are run at an accelerated pace. They usually begin at eight in the morning, end at three-thirty, and, excepting weekends (and sometimes not even them), take place over the course of ten to fifteen consecutive days.

As you might expect, this intensive scheduling serves to underscore and heighten the emotionally loaded nature that is intrinsic to any prison classroom. Consequently, after facilitating six hours of oft-passionate debate about oft-searing autobiographically based stories, I tend to emerge feeling both jazzed and disoriented; wired and strung out on jailhouse adrenaline. This was especially true at the start of my prison career, before I'd learned to shield myself, or at least to try, by donning a thin and all-too-penetrable layer of emotional armor.

But the question of spotty protection aside—and getting back to those unseeing eyes—when class was over those first two years, I would drive down the hill to a sandwich shop. I would eat half a sandwich, sip a cup of coffee, and then, as I came off the last few jolts of the day's prison high, the torpor would set in. I would stare, from my usual corner seat, at the east wall of the restaurant. I would make no attempt to read the batch of student stories that were sitting in my briefcase and were slated for discussion the next day. I didn't even read the newspaper. For half an hour or maybe more, I would simply and vacantly stare.

This was in the city of Monroe back in 1989 and 1990. I remember that at some point during this period, a supervisor at one of the prisons where I taught said, "Robert, you have no idea how much pain you absorb inside that classroom of yours." And if there is indeed a causal relationship between absorption of pain and catatonic behavior, I suppose my supervisor was right. For it was not until the spring of my second year of post-workshop staring that I finally saw what was in front of me. I got out of my seat and walked up to the wall. I carefully studied my find.

It was a map that I'd been staring through, a map. But it wasn't just any map. It was one of those large, rectangular, twenty-four by eighteen inch pictorial souvenir maps that began to appear, during the mid 1980s, in tourist-hungry towns throughout America. These souvenir maps, though not drawn to scale, are brightly colored cheery affairs that are, with regard to density of items, not wholly unlike one of those *"Where's Waldo?"* illustrations. They are jam-packed with people working and playing; with cars, trucks, and scampering dogs; with overpasses, underpasses, rivers, and lakes. They are busy, these maps, very busy.

The 1989 souvenir map of Monroe, which was sponsored by the Sky Valley Chamber of Commerce and funded by a host of downtown merchants, was very much in this bustling mode. A thorough scrutiny of the map reveals thirty-nine office buildings, seventy-three clearly delineated storefronts, sixty-one business signs replete with phone numbers, one bowling alley, seventeen named streets, an old-fashioned locomotive, a set of train tracks, a blue sky, one puffy white cloud, one distant snow-capped mountain, one set of foothills, eighty-five trees, a man on a bicycle, a kid on a skateboard, a farmer plowing, a pruner pruning, sixteen cars, eleven laughing children, one bear, two sheep, and a cow.

In addition, the map includes a Ferris wheel, two tents festooned with waving banners, and an accompanying sign that says "The Evergreen State Fair." Finally, in the midst of all this, the map contains three gold-bordered inserts. The insert at the far left depicts a carousel horse beneath the words, MONROE, THE FAIR CITY, WASHINGTON, 1989. Located adjacent and to the right of the first insert, the second insert is a map within a map, a small scale illustration of western Washington, including the cities of Tacoma, Seattle, and Everett; the state capitol building in Olympia; the snow-covered Olympic and Cascade mountain ranges; two of Washington's four volcanic peaks; and, sitting at the junction of Highways 405 and 2, the city of Monroe, itself.

The third and last insert, which is titled "A Bit of History" and which abuts the blue-purple Skykomish River at the lower right-hand corner of the map, informs us that the first residents of the area were the Snohomish and Skykomish Indians; that white pioneers arrived in the 1800s; that Monroe became an agricultural center as well as a supply stop for miners and loggers; that the city was incorporated in 1902 with a population of 325; and that "since those times, the friendly community has continued to thrive, and its lovely environment and many amenities continue to attract residents, business, and thousands of visitors annually."

Though no reasonable person would make a case for the geographical precision of the 1989 souvenir map of Monroe, there are some who might argue for its figurative truth. And if one is thinking in terms of compressed truth, of a compendium of best case scenarios, perhaps such an argument can be made. If you could, for just one moment, remove all sadness, all illness, all worry, all want, all sinners, and all litter from Monroe; and if, in the same moment, you could capture every business in a prosperous state and every resident in either a highly focused, productive mode, or in a notably carefree frame of mind; and if this emotionally, aesthetically, and economically flawless moment occurred on a gem of a day, on the softest of soft blue-skied days in late August—well then perhaps you'd have a moment such as the one that's depicted in the 1989 map.

But if there is, figuratively speaking, a degree of truth to this map, the map also contains a lie. It is a multifaceted geographical, economic, civic, social, and political lie. And it is, above all, an absurd lie. For the 1989 souvenir map, thick with lore and architectural detail though it is, makes no visual or written representation or allusion to the four state prisons in Monroe.

There are roughly 5,500 non-incarcerated residents of Monroe, and roughly 1,500 incarcerated ones. More than 1,100 people work in the prisons, and though not all of these people live in Monroe, a sizable number do. Moreover, even those prison employees who don't live in Monroe frequent the businesses there.

In addition to the prisons' dramatic demographic impact, there is the matter of their physical presence. The hill on which the three high security institutions are situated looms over downtown Monroe, and, in terms of simple square footage, the prisons dwarf every structure in the city. On clear days, the tall walls of the Reformatory are visible to the myriad east and westbound travelers who drive past Monroe on Route 2. At night, when the prisons are illuminated by giant quartz lights, an orange glow appears in the sky and is visible from many miles away.

I think it is fair to say that the omission of the prisons from the 1989 souvenir map represents an outrageous cartographical lie. But what is the purpose of the lie?

One answer was provided by a spokeswoman for the Sky Valley Chamber of Commerce. When I dropped by the Chamber office to ask the map sponsors about the missing prisons, the spokeswoman pointed out that every business depicted on the map helped to pay for the map's production. When I pointed out, in turn, that it was unlikely that any subsidies had been provided by Highways 2 or 405, by Veterans Memorial Park, or by any other government maintained entity that was, nevertheless, depicted, the Chamber spokeswoman relented. "Well," she said, in reference to the prisons, "they just aren't the sorts of things we'd want to put on our map."

Indeed. Prisons are most definitely not the sorts of things we want to put on our maps, even when they most definitely belong. So what are we to make of Monroe's Bowdlerized souvenir? At first glance, the omission seems almost charming. It's like a wishful lie told by a small, winsome child: ridiculous, laughable, and endearingly transparent.

Upon further reflection, however, one realizes that the map's lie is not merely childlike, colossal, and absurd: it is emblematic, hence instructive. For the Sky Valley Chamber of Commerce is hardly an enigma in its desire to make prisons (and, by extension, prisoners, violence, poverty, hopelessness, the whole prison *gestalt*) disappear. The Chamber's squeamishness about prisons and its prisonless map reflect and embody an acute case of denial that permeates the national psyche.

6 | Going Native

I will call her Mona. Even though she was married, and even though I was married, I was a little in love with her. But I didn't fault myself for that. She was too strong and too alluring to resist. It would be like faulting myself for falling in love with a Siren, and once you've heard that compelling song, a part of you never forgets it. Even now, six years after Mona moved on, I'm still a little in love with her.

Mona's official job title was "Administrative Assistant." But that title was just a cover, a ruse. For Mona's true mission—as almost everyone but the dumbest, most tone deaf guards and the most disengaged administrators perceived—was far more interesting and dangerous. Mona's job was to breathe life into the prison.

She plied her trade in a dazzling manner. She was beautiful. She was brazen. She was unconditionally compassionate. And Mona's sexual energy was preternatural.

"She gets a buzz," a friend of hers told me one day, "whenever she visits The Units [cell blocks]. All those guys in their skivvies, you know."

But mostly she didn't take: she gave. Consider the way Mona dressed. In an assault on the enervating drabness of prison, the clothing she wore was flamboyant. Mona favored loud scarlets and sensual pinks. She wore a jaunty straw hat in the summer. She sported long earrings shaped like tropical birds, and shiny bracelets that jingled and jangled.

Mona's short skirts revealed a fine pair of legs, but Mona wasn't a tramp: far from it. She was a woman, an utter woman, a magnificent piece of work, as all the convicts whom she dressed for understood.

Speaking of convicts, Mona listened to them, which is something prison staffers rarely do. The practice is generally frowned upon. It can lead to accusations of professional drift, of straying into the enemy camp. But that didn't put Mona off. Regardless of a prisoner's crime, no matter how brutal and twisted, she made it her business to lend a sympathetic ear.

And that wasn't all Mona did. She smuggled in cookies and ice cream. She bantered and joked with Crips and with Bloods, with buffed out neo-Nazis, with whomever. And she gave solace to the outcasts: the sex offenders.

The Big Yard would get quiet when Mona walked past. To say she was adored is to put it mildly. Even some of the toughest, most unrepentant cons—men who'd killed just for pleasure and kicks—spoke softly, tenderly, and in reverential tones when the topic of discussion was Mona.

I could go on, of course. I could sing Mona's praises all day. But my aim isn't just to praise Mona: I also want to convey something else. What I want to convey is how Mona screwed up. Screwed up royally, in fact. Fucked up big-time. And once the carnage was over; once the curtain came down; once Mona's blinding luminescence was extinguished, I sat down at my desk and betrayed a woman I loved by writing this story about her.

Going Native

a story by Robert Ellis Gordon

WELL THEY HIRED THIS MONA to run the new library, the library with hardly any books. You see, they decided it's a good thing to teach us criminals how to read so that if, by any chance, we ever get released, we can fill out a job application. But on the other hand, what with the tight fiscal times and the current anti-rehabilitation sentiment, they didn't want to go overboard on us scums. So our keepers came up with a compromise solution: they agreed to pay for new shelves and a full-time librarian, but in fairness to all the more deserving law-abiding citizens out there, they drew the line at purchasing new books.

Still, even without any books except for a few boring dog-eared paperbacks that were donated by some well-meaning Christians, it's a pleasant place to visit, Mona's library. For one thing she keeps the coffee pot going all day long. Also, she commits a Class B felony on a regular basis, which is to say she smuggles in contraband in the form of delicious homemade molasses cookies. In addition, she knows how to listen sympathetically, which is a rare and for the most part welcome attribute in a place like this. The only reason I say "for the most part" is because she insists on treating *everyone* the same, even the outcasts who the rest of us wouldn't be caught dead sitting at the same table with in the chow hall, let alone lending a friendly ear to. You know who I mean—the Chesters, the child molesters.

But that's Mona's style, equal treatment. In fact she even takes it a step further and actually *empathizes* with the bastards, actually imagines herself in their shoes. Oh sure, she has children of her own, a boy and two little girls who she would sacrifice her life for in an instant; who she would die to protect, no regrets. But then again, she thinks to herself as she listens to yet another Chester pour out his pathetic, disgusting story—then again, Mona has to admit, her own sexual preference, her interest in males, was established early on. In fact, she recalls, it was firmly ingrained by the age of eleven or twelve. So who is she, she explains to her less enlightened friends over coffee one Saturday morning in her kitchen—with the sunlight streaming in and the kids out back kicking a soccer ball and the smell of a turkey roasting in the oven—who is she, Mona asks, to sit in judgment?

Tsk tsk, think her friends who are, themselves, the mothers of small children. Watch out, Mona, they are thinking. Those beasts are in prison for a reason, you know. Now don't be going native, they warn her.

And as for us non-sex crime guys, us robbers and forgers and drug dealing murderers, us garden variety scums? How do *we* respond to Mona's compassion? We shrug our shoulders and do our best to overlook it. After all, as I say, it's just Mona's style, this excessive degree of tolerance. Besides, in here you forgive any woman who's even moderately attractive, let alone drop dead gorgeous. And you don't have to worry, our Mona is safe, even around notorious rapos. Because if anyone lays a *finger* on our favorite librarian, he'll get a shiv in the gizzard in no time.

Well you can imagine the tremors of pleasure and pain that course through our little prison when Mona comes waltzing in. How happy we are to see her arrive at work in the morning! And how still and quiet we become inside when she goes home for the night, especially on those soft warm evenings in June and July when the sun seems to linger on the horizon forever, the evenings of the endless dusk. I wish you could see the way our Mona literally sashays out—past the checkpoints, past the dicks with their mace cans and guns, past the entrance to the cell blocks where we sleep, in some cases for just a few years, in others for the rest of our lives—and then she finally disappears into the dark, forbidden tunnel which leads to the other side. And she does it in a pink dress and a straw hat of all things. Yes, a straw hat, I tell you. In a prison! Sauntering out with that pink dress shifting ever so slightly in the light summer breeze, and all of us standing around in the Big Yard, pausing for just a second to forget where we are, to forget who we are, to forget about the things we did to get here; to forget, if only briefly, about shanks in the back or about that demented cellmate we once had, the psycho who we actually found devouring his own excrement at four o'clock on one horrible morning. Not to mention what it feels like when you're strapped down in the chair with shaved legs, a shaved head, and a man-sized diaper—well as I say, for a moment we forget about that and just stand in the Big Yard and stare.

But here I am talking about horizons and dusks and Mona's kitchen on a Saturday morning. As if I could see such things! It's pure speculation, nothing more. I haven't been inside a house for eleven years. And as for this business of horizons—well you try spotting the line where the sky meets the earth by peering through a solid concrete wall. Go ahead, give it a try. And don't feel too bad when you fail miserably. I'll bet Houdini himself couldn't do it! And even if Houdini could, Houdini wouldn't hang around a prison. I mean, aside from the fact that Houdini is dead, why would a fellow with his aptitude for escape even bother to spend one night with our cockroaches? The answer, of course, is he wouldn't.

But what's Houdini got to do with all of this? The point is that for the rest of us non-Houdini types, the most we can see is a cloud. Or an airplane, perhaps, or a bird passing by. And with regard to our dawns and dusks—well once those floodlights go on in the late afternoon, all celestial colors disappear. No streaks of pink or orange for us scums! In fact, in the glare of those merciless lights, the very notion of sky disappears. No stars, no moon: the sky doesn't exist, except, in our minds, as an idea.

Still, I like imagining the sky at the edge of the day, tinged with purple, vermilion, and gold. And I like to think of the glow from a red setting sun glinting off the blue ice of an ancient glacier. And of a cream-colored moon, a fat cream-colored moon, slowly rising over tall mountain peaks; casting its light on the valleys and slopes and the meadows where bear and elk forage; and where, I have heard, silver wolves have returned, running softly, like ghosts, through the night.

That's one thing I want to see if I ever get out: a wolf, a wild wolf, running free. And the kaleidoscopic city of Las Vegas. Also, with luck, if there are any zebras left, a zebra galloping on the African veldt. As I often remark to Noodle, my friend, on our evenings strolls around the Yard, that's what Mona's sensuality, her raw sexual power, often makes me think of: a zebra.

But Noodle takes issue with this comparison. He says a zebra is too gamey for our Mona. She's more like a dolphin, he says; soft and playful and friendly to men. Consider her laugh, Noodle says.

And while I have to admit that Mona has a playful laugh, a zebra is exotic, I point out. A zebra has stripes. It's *alive.* And what is Mona but life in a dead place like this with that straw hat she wears in the summer? And those eye-burning scarlets she wears in the winter, not to mention her flamingo-shaped earrings. Yes, flamingo-shaped earrings, I tell you. In a prison, no less. Just outrageous! They're bright pink with wide wings and they drape her fine neck, Mona's thin, soft, exquisite white neck. A zebra wakes you, I say. A dolphin lulls you to sleep.

So it goes back and forth, this debate: zebras, Houdini, the news of the day, such as Mona's latest prize: an encyclopedia. God knows where she snared the ragged thing. It's mildewed and the "B" volume is missing. Also, it's old, it's so frozen in time that JFK is still the handsome, witty president. But at least it's something new for us to read.

We continue to walk around the crushed cinder track that encircles the Big Prison Yard. We pass the familiar sights you've all seen, the ones they show you on those late night TV movies: the weight lifting crowd with their biker tattoos, cussing and spitting for all they're worth. And the Crips and the Bloods and those neo-Nazi folks, posturing and glowering for each other. And see, over there, that convict staring at the wall? What's the fellow looking at? A bug. Yes, he's discovered an exotic breed of earwig! But no, it turns out on closer inspection, it's just a standard beetle after all. Nothing special to write home about, the fellow thinks. Still, the bug is alive and might make a fine pet. Will it do tricks, the fellow wonders. What should he name it?

But you know about this from watching TV; you know the only pets in here are insects. And then there are the things you don't know. For example, the word, "defleured." What could it possibly mean? That fine sounding word that rolls off your tongue, so soft and poetic: *defleured.*

Well, I'll tell you exactly what it means. It's what the brothers here say after raping a fish, a fresh virgin fish who's just arrived. They say the pretty young boy has now been defleured.

There is so much they don't show you on TV! For instance...but wait...hear that hush setting in? Note how our hard convict eyes are growing soft? And see, over there, that flash of straw hat? Yes, our Mona is leaving for the night. She came in at ten-thirty to open the library and now it's past seven o'clock. So it's time to go home and tuck the kids into bed, do the deed with her husband, and so forth.

But why isn't our Mona in a hurry? Why does she dawdle at the checkpoints? And twirl around slowly as she approaches the gate, and then linger at the entrance to the forbidden tunnel? Why spend so much as an extra second in this place?

Well it doesn't take a genius to solve this riddle. See how she turns her back on the tunnel, faces out on the Big Yard and smiles?

See her stick her index finger in her mouth? Our Mona licks it like she'd lick an ice cream cone. Then she removes the wet finger from her mouth and runs it ever so slowly down her dress; past the lovely right bosom, pausing briefly near the navel, and inching over to a provocative flaring hip.

Yes, you know what our Mona is up to. She is giving us a picture to take back to our cells, a gift to keep us company for the night. If only I were a real writer! What a tale I would weave about these Monas; these hundreds of Monas we take back to our cells, each one a different Mona, but still a Mona.

For some she becomes the devoted lover we never had, the one who showers our face with her kisses; who weeps as she calls us "my sweet darling pumpkin;" who vows to never leave us no matter what; no matter who we killed to get into this place, no matter how long we'll be here.

For others, she's a hellcat of a lover. Her nails draw blood; she knows every position. She could've written the book on giving pleasure!

And for still others, alas, our Mona is a victim who gets tied up and handcuffed and whipped. And even worse things occur in those cells, things I refuse to put on paper. But you can spare your clucking tongues for something else. This is prison, dear reader, not life! Mona gives us a gift and I love her for that and so does Jesus, I'll bet, and even Mary. And who cares if our Mona gets off on all this? Oh, you can tell she feels some tingles as she poses. But God doesn't mind a few harmless pleasant tingles: He has more important matters to condemn.

Or so, at any rate, say I. But getting back to Mona, she turns around slowly and disappears through the dark forbidden tunnel. And what do we do, us dangerous felons, us lonely and pathetic convict scums? We just stand there, breathing softly, saying nothing.

A year goes by. It is marked by disagreeable events. One day in the chow hall, for example, one convict scum attacks another convict scum for chewing a banana too loudly. "I can't stand the sound of mushy bananas. I hate that fucking sound!" the attacker screams. Then George—that's his name, the banana hating fellow. He's a good friend of Noodle's and mine. Well anyway, this George, he pounces on the guy; he throws the loud chewer to the floor. He pummels him for making mushy sounds. And that's just the start of George's outburst. Because then—catch this—George scoops out an eye. Yes, he rips out the chewer's left eyeball! And he eats the damned thing, just gobbles it down, as if it were an after dinner mint.

Naturally, George gets sent to the hole. We haven't heard from our friend for several months. And we don't expect him to emerge, if he ever emerges, until he's spent several years down in lock-up; until he's spent several years being chained to a wall, being walked on a leash, and so forth.

It was a blue eye, in case you were wondering. And the whole business did a number on Noodle: he's been in a bad mood ever since. For instance, on our walks around the crushed cinder track, if I bring up the subject of wolves—of the wild wolves I hope to see if I get out—Noodle gives me a look of disdain. "Dream on, my friend," Noodle says. "There aren't any wild wolves left. Or for that matter mountains. Or for that matter trees. It's all K-Marts and malls out there."

Of course I know Noodle's lying about the K-Marts and malls; I just know there are mountains out there. Still, I can't know for certain because I can't see them. What I'd give for a glimpse, just one tiny glimpse, of a frigid, wind-blown, icy, snow-capped peak!

So as I say, it's been a difficult year. But the worst news is yet to come. For what are eyeballs and K-Marts compared to Mona? And as you've probably guessed, our favorite librarian, our favorite pocket of light, is growing dim. Her spirits are sagging. It happens. How could it not happen in a dead place like this? Consider all the pain she absorbs. And then consider the fact that she isn't a sponge, and that even if she is, a sponge has limits.

But this isn't a treatise on sponges! I'm merely saying that our Mona is burning out. The usual symptoms are present: the droop in her shoulders, the unfocused glazed eyes, the way she trudges instead of sauntering as she used to. Not to mention the symptom that hurts us the most: the decline in her listening skills. Mona no longer wishes to hear our life stories; about all the abuse we endured; about the traumas that caused us to do our bad deeds, or how messed up we were when we did them. And when we bend her ear just the same—when we list our excuses—she retreats to a secret place; to a zone in her mind that no convict can reach.

Well, we've seen such retreats before. An outsider comes in and goes numb from the onslaught. It's just a matter of time before she quits. Tomorrow, perhaps, or maybe next week. A month at the absolute outside.

Or so it is generally assumed. But then, one day...what's this? The old Mona, herself, has returned. It's the old Mona, but even moreso if you can believe it.

What a flurry of activity is taking place! After ages without a batch of homemade molasses cookies, Mona goes to town in her kitchen. Suddenly we're deluged not only with molasses cookies but with sugar and peanut butter cookies as well. And with semi-sweet chocolate chips, my favorite. Then one Friday in June she goes way out on a limb: she smuggles in Haagen-Daaz ice cream. It's quite soupy, as you might expect, by the time we get it. But we drink it down like greedy children as we sit in the library. We savor the rich creamy taste. Then we pat our bloated tummies. We are filled with good cheer. We are lazy and happy. Contented.

That Haagen-Daaz party was impressive. It takes guts to smuggle ice cream in a book bag. But even more remarkable than smuggling stuff which, if it drips through your book bag can get you fired, is the complete transformation of our librarian's face. What a glow she exudes! So much radiance! And peace and serenity, goodwill and all that. In addition, the straw hat is back. We haven't seen the festive hat for several months. But Mona's wearing it again, and at a jaunty new angle.

Of course we understand what this indicates. It points to one thing and one thing only. But the question that haunts us is who. Which convict scum is our Mona in love with? Which convict scum has won the prize? With whom is she exchanging secret letters and looks? Whose soul has she picked to destroy? For as I say, this is prison, not life. And make no mistake: love will kill you in here.

But getting back to Mona's choice: it's Jimmy Ellis. How can we tell? We have eyes. We know this man behind the lines. We note the signs. Just look at the fool lying flat on his bunk with that beatific smile on his face. He is staring up at cobwebs, rusty pipes, and prison grime as if he's witnessing a vision of the Holy Mother! The moron lies there, entranced, for hours. And he used to be well thought of, Jimmy Ellis. Jimmy Ellis killed a cop. He had respect.

Now he's soused on endorphins. Pathetic. But more pathetic by far than exuding dumb bliss is the way he responds—or should I say doesn't respond—to a fresh fish who takes his seat in the chow hall. It happens one day at lunch. And love struck or not, this calls for action. You see, a convict with respect has a certain seat at a certain table, and no one but no one is allowed to take that seat, especially not a fresh fish.

So does Jimmy knock the kid's teeth out like he ought to? Or sell the kid's ass to some horny prison bulldog, or make arrangements for a tragic, fatal accident? No, Jimmy Ellis does not. He just shrugs and lets the kid keep on eating. And to make matters worse he walks his tray to a table where several known Chesters are sitting. And he joins them for lunch, yes he *talks* to those guys, actually makes idle chitchat with the scums!

It's enough to make all of us old-timers puke, Jimmy's newfound broadmindedness regarding perverts. We cringe with vicarious shame. But at least his insufferable generosity of spirit will be a blessedly short-lived phenomenon. That's the one saving grace: his bliss can't last. For what goes up must come down, as the saying goes. And by down, I mean down: a bottomless pit.

The first thing to set in will be jealousy. It's always the first thing in situations like this, and when it hits, it hits hard, and for good reason. See, Jimmy will realize that he has lots of rivals—roughly twelve hundred in the joint. Less a few genuine homosexuals. But even subtracting the hardcore queers, that's still a lot of straight men in one place; a God-awful ratio of unattached males to the one attractive female in our midst. And never mind the fact that twelve hundred felons aren't out to steal Mona from Jimmy Ellis. Whoever said jealousy is rational?

But to continue with the demons that will arise: he'll also start to think about Mona's husband. He'll imagine the fellow banging his bitch. He'll assume they go at it every night. He'll assume they go at it *all night* every night, and yes I know, marriage isn't like that. But try imparting that knowledge to Jimmy Ellis. Try telling anything to anyone who's locked up and in love. And Jimmy Ellis isn't in here for the weekend. The man killed a cop; the man is down for life without. So chances are, he'll go crazy soon enough.

And as for us spectators, what do we do while we're waiting for Mona's chosen one to crack? How do we fritter away the hours? We talk about the scandal, of course. Why Jimmy Ellis, we wonder. Why not handsome Mick Smith? Or deep, brooding Noodle? Or for that matter, me? What's so special about Jimmy Ellis, we'd like to know.

Or is Jimmy Ellis beside the point, as Noodle ventures. In his opinion, Jimmy Ellis is irrelevant. "It's her marriage," he says. "It's on the rocks."

"Why's that?" I say.

"She's bored," Noodle says as we pass by the weight lifting crowd. "She can't hack straight life anymore."

I think about this as we circle the track, scrunching crushed cinder beneath our feet. I think maybe Noodle's onto something. I begin to have a vision of Mona's other life, of what it's like when she gets home from the office. I see her sitting with her husband after dinner. The kids are out back playing tetherball. And Bill—that's his name, the name I choose for Mona's husband—either Bill or Vince or Bert, or maybe Dick. Well anyway, Bill has a dilemma: should he borrow or not borrow the neighbor's gas powered edger? On the plus side of the equation there's aesthetics. "An edged lawn just looks nicer," Bill says. "Who can argue with a nice squared up edge?"

"But on the downside," he continues, and he proceeds to delineate the negative aspects of lawn edging, e.g. upkeep, to name one example. It's a once a month chore, he predicts. Plus the investment involved if he buys his own edger, and let's face facts, Bill points out, there's no avoiding it. After all, he can't borrow indefinitely. "You just don't *do* that to a neighbor," he states emphatically. So in conclusion, he says as he nods like a sage and gazes into the eyes of his beloved, it's a textbook case of a split decision, of six of one versus half a dozen of the other. "Know what I mean, honey?" he says.

"Mmm," Mona says, noncommittally. Then she excuses herself to go to the bathroom where she sits on the toilet and weeps. She is thinking about eaten eyeballs. And about the meaning of the word *defleured*. She wipes her eyes and turns her thoughts to a short, smuggled letter, the latest missive she's received from Jimmy Ellis. It's the one about the smell of her hair. He said he'd smelled it one day in the Reference Section; that he'd gotten a fleeting if overpowering whiff of Mona's shoulder length auburn hair. He'd never smelled such a smell before. It made him dizzy, he said. It made him see God.

Mona thinks about Jimmy's life sentence. Her quiet weeping turns into sobbing. She sobs loudly enough for her husband to hear, so Vince—I mean Bill—knocks on the door. "What's the matter, cupcake?" he says.

Well, what's she supposed to say? How can she possibly talk to a man whose *raison d'être* is home improvement? I mean the matter of Jimmy Ellis aside, Mona's married to a man who actually believes that government officials don't lie! So how can she open her heart to this fool; how can she say what's on her mind? *I.e.* her fantasy regarding the sex doc. You know, the hotshot psychologist with all the degrees, the one who treats our court-certified perverts.

He makes them jerk off out loud, this doctor does. Yes, there's a room, so we're told, a subterranean room, in the southwest wing of our little prison, with one-way glass looking in and lots of Kleenex near at hand. The room is used for state-funded masturbation. Not that anyone thinks the cure works. Not that anyone with half a lousy brain in their head gives any credence to aversion therapy. In fact, studies *prove* it's a waste of tax dollars.

But this isn't a critique of public policy! I'm merely describing the sex doctor's methods, merely stating the sick, juicy truth. To wit, the good doctor treats a Chester molester by making him shout out the pictures; by making him blab the disgusting, filthy pictures he conjures while jerking off. And then, at the moment—the critical juncture, the timeless pause before the Chester shoots his wad—the good doctor applies years of specialized training by either squirting ammonia up the poor bastard's nose, or by shocking him, electrically, in the scrotum.

Imagine treating perverts for a living! It's a profession for creeps, Mona thinks. Which is why Mona wishes that once, just once, the creepy doctor could get a taste of his own medicine. Yes, she'd wave her magic wand and all the shouting would cease—the Chester's shouting, that is. A silence follows. And then, against his will, not knowing what drives him, what mysterious compulsion has taken hold, the hotshot doctor unbuckles his belt. And there in the room, in front of his client, the doctor starts flogging *his* dolphin. And shouting the pictures he sees in *his* head.

Oh, the scene would be delicious, so delicious. There would be boots, whips, and chains in abundance. And allusions to melons and sheep. Every sick, twisted thought, every kinky possibility—including children and mashed potatoes—would be mentioned. And the unifying theme, Mona's good instincts tell her, the tie that binds these rabid fantasies together, would be desire for dominance, desire to hurt.

Well just once, as I say, she'd like to see it. Mona smiles at the prospect. She almost laughs. But then she starts thinking about Jimmy's fine shoulders, about how much she longs to touch them. She aches for Jimmy. So now she's on the verge of sobbing again, of letting loose with a cathartic, primal wail. But before she has a chance to vent her despair, Mona's lawn-care obsessed, risk-aversive flabby husband knocks on the door again. "What's going on?" he implores. "What's wrong?"

Mona stifles her wail and shakes her head. Oh, how she wishes that she could wave her magic wand and erase the last fifteen years—the marriage, the mortgage, the car payments, all that. But of course there's no such thing as magic wands. Besides, Vince—I mean Bill—well he may lack fine shoulders, but he does draw a handsome salary. And dull as dishwater though he is, he has good intentions. Not to mention the most important responsibility of all: raising their three precious kids; keeping them safe in this crime riddled world.

Mona's stuck with her life, alright. She briefly wishes she had terminal cancer. Then she takes a deep breath and stands up. She washes her face at the sink. She wipes it dry, sighs again, and emerges from the bathroom.

"What is it?" Bill says. "What's the matter?"

"PMS," Mona says. "I'm sorry, I'm—"

"Hey, it's okay," Bill says. He has read about PMS in *Reader's Digest*. "It's hormones, that's all. Just hormones." He gives Mona a hug, a non-sexual hug, the type intended to let her know he understands. And Mona accepts it, she leans into his hug, she lets him think that he's being a comfort.

This is excellent for Bill's self-esteem. But later, in bed, in the dark, making love, as Mona's nails rip into his back, she blurts a strange name. "Jimmy Jimmy," she says. "Oh *Jimmy!*" she cries as she comes.

Who's Jimmy? Bill wonders. He wants to ask. But he's also afraid to ask, so he says nothing.

And as for our hero, the demented cop killer? How is *he* faring these days? Well, he's providing us with first-rate entertainment. One minute he's raving about the smell of Mona's hair, how it's exactly like God, and so forth. The next minute, reality sets in. He curls into a ball, a tight fetal ball, as he considers his prospects for getting laid; as it occurs to Jimmy Ellis that that whiff of her hair may be as close as he'll ever get to touching Mona. Then his eyes fill with hate as he broods about his rivals, about those aforementioned twelve hundred felons. But soon his crazy eyes soften as he contemplates Mona, the smell of her hair, etc.

It's quite a show, as I say, and it's becoming perilous. You see, it's illegal for a convict to have feelings in here, to have feelings for a staff member, that is. You don't believe me? Look it up: it's in The Code. But to continue, our lovebird has become so transparent that the snitches, who've been trying to stir up trouble for weeks, are no longer being scoffed at by the dicks. So now the dicks are watching Jimmy and Mona. And this means, in turn, no more contraband letters, no more meaningful gazes across the library, no more hair sniffing orgies in the Reference Section. No more monkey business, period, is what it means. Because if Jimmy is caught he'll be shipped off in chains to live out his days in a dungeon. Yes, that's what they do when one of us scums is found guilty of having illegal feelings: they trundle him off to die alone in Walla Walla, a most hideous prison by all accounts.

Of course nerves are frayed around here. Jimmy Ellis is scared. Even Mona is scared, and our Mona, as you've no doubt surmised by now, is as fearless as the hardest of hardcore grizzled convict scums. Still, she's scared about what might happen to Jimmy Ellis. Plus she's heard a few rumors that make her fear for the snitches. Not that she likes snitches: she's on our side. But she's heard that her boyfriend is making some noises about having his friends take them out. And if Jimmy's pals do the deed, if they shank a few snitches, all that blood will be on her hands. So what does our heroine elect to do? What any stressed out, love-sick woman would do. Yes, she seeks the advice of a psychic.

Now this psychic, a reader of tea leaves and cards, was on the up and up, Noodle claims. It seems that Noodle and Mona had a brief, furtive chat as he checked out a book one day. And according to what Noodle said Mona told him, she confessed what we already knew. *I.e.* she told Noodle about her passion for Jimmy Ellis, about her foundering marriage, etc. Plus, he continued, she'd sought out this psychic, the one with the sterling reputation. And this psychic had a horrifying vision. The psychic trembled and quaked when she read Mona's cards. She turned an otherworldly pale. She blanched.

"What is it?" Mona said, but the psychic just groaned. The psychic rocked back and forth. She closed her eyes.

"What do you see?" Mona asked.

"I see two murdered people," said the psychic.

"Murdered?" said Mona.

The psychic shuddered again. Then she spoke in a strange distant voice; a voice that seemed to come from outside the room, from some deep, dark, dank hole in the ground. "This man who you love— his name is Jimmy, I think—this man will be killed," said the psychic. "And the forces who kill him, who take his spirit away, will also, I fear, do you in."

Or so I imagined the scene with the gypsy as Noodle recounted the conversation. "The psychic really said that? She'll get killed?"

"Well, pretty close," Noodle said. "The psychic said her spirit will be snuffed. That she'll run out of reasons for being alive, and that she'll spend her life *wishing* she was dead."

We passed by the Crips and then we passed by the Bloods. "So why doesn't she leave?" I said. "Why doesn't she quit her job?"

Noodle shrugged. "Search me," he said.

December. The snow we can't see in the mountains we can't see provides a thick cozy blanket for the hibernating bears. All is muffled and white up there. The silver wolves run beneath the moon we can't see. In my dreams I hear their howls as I float beside them. In my dreams I howl with them. They are my friends.

And what do I hear when I'm awake? I hear Jimmy Ellis howling in the infirmary. It's a six bed affair, our little prison's little infirmary. And wouldn't you know, it's just a few yards away, it's literally *next door* to Mona's library. Inside the infirmary they're force-feeding Jimmy. They're shoving vitamins and minerals up his veins. They're introducing amino acids into the poor shackled bastard.

So that's one thing I hear: Jimmy's howls. In addition I hear frost-hardened cinder beneath my feet. It makes a sharp, snappy, no-nonsense sound. And I hear Noodle spouting off about some ancient fairy tale, about the lies we tell our children about some emperor. You know which emperor: the one with no clothes.

It's morning in the joint, by the way. Yes, we've taken to walking after breakfast. And after lunch and after dinner as well. We walk without gloves, we walk in thin socks, we walk all day long in the mean winter air. Our digits turn numb, but so what? Anything's better than sitting in the library and staring at our Mona's ravaged face.

"It's such a fucking lie!" Noodle's saying. He's acting quite indignant about that fairy tale. "Know what I mean?" he says. "Some kid tells the truth about those tailors. Some kid says the Big Cheese got swindled. Some kid makes a fool out of all the top dogs, out of all the chief ministers of this and that, and we're asked to believe that the bozos *reward* him. Bullfuckingshit!" Noodle says. "They'd hang the kid up by his toes. They'd hang him at the gate by the moat. Then they'd cut off his dong as a warning. They'd stuff his dong and his balls in his mouth. And then, after that, they'd slice up his family. That's the true fucking story!" Noodle says.

I'm doing my best to ignore him. But don't get me wrong, I'm not being rude. It's just not my style, being rude. Ask anyone here, I'm always a gentleman. I haven't made a rude remark in eleven years. I've been on my best behavior since killing my man, a man whose face I can't even remember.

The man whose face I can't remember stole my woman. I can't remember the woman's face, either. I do, however, remember her name. It was Hilda if you can believe it. *Hilda.* Imagine being named Hilda in this day and age. What a name for a woman to go to prison for!

But that's neither here nor there. The point, as I was saying, is that Noodle doesn't care if I'm doing my best to ignore him. It's when he's quiet that you ought to pay attention. He's just making a fuss to keep the demons at bay, to stop himself from dwelling on the inevitable.

And what is the inevitable demon? It's Mona's last day at work today. It's her last day inside our little prison. She'll arrive and she'll leave and she'll never return.

We pass by the weightlifting crowd. We pass by the Crips, the Bloods, and the neo-Nazis. We pass blind Kevin and old Edgar in his wheelchair. *Everyone's* turned out to see what comes down. Hell, there's even a gaggle of Chesters. See them huddled around the metal detector, thinking their vile Chester thoughts?

We lower our eyes as we walk by the scums. To nod hello could have adverse consequences. Then we pass by the entrance to the hole. Somewhere down there our friend George resides, being walked on a leash and so forth, while up here on earth we walk without leashes.

In the distance Jimmy howls. A fog descends. We convicts grow dim and then vanish in the stuff, pale beings on our way to full-fledged ghosthood.

You think I'm making this up but I'm not. It's perfectly normal to have fog in December, and as for our Mona—what happened to her—well that, too, is easy to explain. How she fell from prison grace, I mean. Why she had to quit her job in a hurry.

Mona's downfall, like Richard M. Nixon's before her, was the indiscriminate use of technology. Of audio technology, to be precise. You see, she made a cassette of her session. She recorded that hour with the reader of cards and brought the tape home in her handbag. Then she tucked the cassette in a drawer. Tucked it deep down inside of her underwear drawer, slipped it in with her soft magic dainties.

Next Vince—I mean Bill—got ahold of it. His mind drifted, one day, from lawn edging to bras, and that's all she wrote, so to speak.

Too bad the guy was a fetishist. Too bad he played that cassette. A terrible shame he gave Mona a choice, a bad choice which means simply no good choice. "It's Jimmy Ellis," he said, "or me and the kids. One or the other. Not both."

She said, "What were you doing in my underwear drawer?"

"It's either him or your kids," Bill said.

Or so she told Noodle, who told me. And that's where things stood when she gave notice. The dicks, of course, were gleeful at the prospect. Some of them started to lick their chops; some of them actually drooled. And I do not mean metaphorically. Inside their minds I could see the saliva. I saw jugs of the stuff spilling over.

And why not see jugs full of spit? It was a perfectly logical vision. For the instant she leaves they'll haul Jimmy away to languish in the dungeon called Walla Walla. Jimmy knows it, Mona knows it, the whole joint knows the score. And misery is what makes dicks ecstatic.

Or most dicks, at any rate, in my experience. But getting back to the story: as soon as Mona gave notice, Jimmy stopped eating and drinking. He just lay on his bunk and lost weight. He just lay there and stared for a week.

He was making a romantic statement. A self-serving romantic statement. For in addition to saying "I love you" to Mona, he was hoping to die in the process, thereby avoiding the next forty years. But the dicks are too cunning to let him do that. I mean just imagine if everyone did. The whole notion of dungeons would turn into a mockery, and the chair would become obsolete. Plus the dicks would be unemployed. Hence refusal of nourishment is a serious infraction: it's strictly against The Code. And that explains why Jimmy's chained to a bed, why he's plugged up with tubes and howling.

I know what you're thinking out there in the world. I can picture your smug incredulity. But what do you know about anything? This is prison, my friends. Strange things happen in here.

Yet so do normal things, they really do. Even if they happen a few hours late. Take that normal thing called sunrise. Well, that's what's occurring at this moment. The sun is making it's way above the tall concrete wall, and the grim fog of December breaks apart. Then, at long last, our Mona walks in. She isn't wearing her thick winter coat. Or her blue woolen hat. Or her plush furry mittens. No, she's wearing that pink cotton dress. Her goddamned pink dress. And sandals. Yes sandals, I tell you, on Christmas Eve Day. And her jaunty straw hat. How nice!

We stand there and sniff as she sashays across, strides right into our little prison's infirmary. She's never done that before, walked into the infirmary. We stand there surprised, on guard. We stop sniffing, long distance, up the slits of her dress, beneath the straps in the back, and so forth. We just stand there and wait for what happens.

And then, as it happens, I see it unfold. I don't mean I imagine the scene. What I mean is I see through a crack in reality, the way Houdini might've seen if he'd been here. But Houdini wouldn't stay here, as I've mentioned. He wouldn't spend a single night with our cockroaches. Thus it's all up to me to be the only true witness. It's my job to report. I see that now.

So here's my report: not much happens. She goes up to Jimmy's bed. "I love you," she mouths.

"I love you," he mouths.

Then Mona leaves. Walks out past the dicks with their mace cans and guns; past the entrance to the cell blocks where we sleep; and finally, inexorably, into the dark forbidden tunnel where she's transported, like an angel, to the other side.

7 | Peering into the Funhouse Mirror

by Robert Ellis Gordon

I N A PLACE WHERE despair often reached toxic levels, it was always a pleasure to encounter a student who had an unquenchable zest for life. One I remember with particular fondness was an utterly unrepentant armed robber. During the course of his felonious career he'd robbed banks, 7-Elevens, and other establishments throughout California and the Pacific Northwest. This robber was a handsome son of a gun with twinkling eyes and a mischievous grin. You could tell he was a real lady killer.

When the robber took my creative writing workshop, he wrote a highly amusing step-by-step primer on how to establish an alias. The robber's MO was quite inventive. He'd land in a new town, visit a local graveyard, and find the tombstone of a man who was born at about the same time he was. Then, through a series of clever maneuvers, the robber would adopt the dead man's identity. He would obtain a social security card and even a driver's license bearing the dead man's name.

Once his new alias was established, the robber would ply his trade secure in the knowledge that if he was ever pulled over for a traffic violation, no outstanding arrest warrants would appear on the police computer. After committing a string of holdups—but before the cops closed in—the robber would steal a car, drive to a new town, visit a local graveyard, establish a brand new identity, and ply his trade again.

It took several years and some thorough police work, but the law finally caught up with the robber. When he was arrested, the robber had in excess of twenty aliases. At his trial, the robber was found guilty of committing a large number of hold-ups under a wide assortment of names. When it came time for sentencing, the judge couldn't figure out who the robber really was. Consequently, he was ordered to serve a long prison term under one of his assumed names.

In his step-by-step primer on how to establish an alias, the robber claimed that having so many identities was a real boon in prison. He pointed out that when some convict yells a friendly greeting to another convict in the Big Yard, the name that is hollered is frequently one of his many aliases. Therefore, on the off chance that the convict who's doing the hollering is an old acquaintance from the streets, the robber always stops and returns the greeting. Ninety-nine times out of a hundred, of course, the convict who's doing the hollering is hollering at someone else. But the robber is the easygoing sort who most people take a shine to. In this way, he claimed, he made lots of friends, and never suffered from loneliness in prison.

After reading the amusing how-to primer, I felt badly that this self-possessed, witty, and charming fellow would have to fritter away years in prison. But sympathy wasn't all I felt: I was also a bit envious of the man.

Such envy may seem odd. After all, I got to leave the prison every day. I had my freedom. Still, like many writers, I tend to be morose, introspective, and anxious. So my freedom notwithstanding, I knew that I could never, no matter how hard I tried, extract an *iota* of the fun and joy that the handsome and charming if incarcerated robber somehow managed to milk out of life.

■ ■ ■

His name was Orlock, Victor Orlock. You probably wouldn't like him. He had a soft, pulpy handshake; he was shaped like a pear; he didn't take showers; and he had a very serious case of body odor. His hair was greasy, his skin was greasy, and his pudgy face was riddled with pimples.

Orlock fashioned himself to be an intellectual, and though I suspected he wasn't as well read as he claimed, he clearly had access to a thesaurus. He used lots of big words in the stories he wrote, although you really couldn't call them stories. They were musings, I guess, philosophical musings about trite metaphysical questions. (Does God exist/do souls really die/what is reality/blah-blah-blah.) He never came up with anything original or deep. He was, from my vantage point as editor/teacher, avoiding his emotionally powerful stories by hiding behind an intellectual mask.

And Orlock was a loser. Boy, was he a loser. In a classroom filled with society's losers, with society's most reviled individuals, it required only one look around to get a sense of the pecking order; to ascertain that Orlock had no allies or friends, that he was clearly the biggest loser of the bunch. I never read his "jacket"—his criminal history—and there was never any need to do so. I knew for a fact, the moment I met him (I never shook his pulpy hand again) that he was an incurable child molester. "Baby Rapers," as child molesters are known in prison, often practice poor personal hygiene. And the passage of time only served to underscore my initial diagnosis of Orlock's crime. For I'd noticed, after teaching inside for several years, that the stories composed by hard-wired pedophiles tend to be maddeningly elliptical.

Orlock, in short, was repugnant. But I was his teacher, and my mandate, whether I liked him or not, was to help him become a better writer. I started by urging him to avoid the use of gratuitously esoteric language. (A student in class once put it more bluntly: "Hundred dollar words don't mean shit," he said, looking at Orlock, not me. I can't remember the student's name or face, but I frequently thank him in my thoughts. For whenever I catch myself coasting along in a slick, self-indulgent mode, I hear that student calling bullshit on me, and I respond by attempting to grapple with the subject I'm using stylistic flimflam to avoid.)

As for Orlock, I informed him that if he wanted to be profound, the profundity must *emerge* from his stories. I said it cannot be imposed from without. Jesus often spoke in parables, I pointed out, and he did so for good reason. Talking down to one's listeners by preaching abstractions is as ill-advised a strategy for a Messiah to follow as it is for a candidate for town alderman. Condescending preaching causes people to recoil, and, ultimately, to reject the speaker. But Jesus had a few tricks up his sleeve, and knew something that Orlock didn't: we humans are suckers for stories. Hence, if one wants to impart a moral or a theme, one must weave it, in a manner that is subtle and deft, into the fabric of a mesmerizing tale.

I challenged Orlock, again and again, to summon the courage to make himself vulnerable; to stop hiding behind the mask of intellectual superiority; and to write simply-worded stories from the heart.

This was at the Pine Lodge Prison, a minimum security facility for offenders who have less than three years to go on their sentences. During the day, Pine Lodge offers literacy, job training, and other such programs designed to prepare its residents, some of whom have spent more than twenty years in maximum security institutions, for re-entry into the outside world. Classes such as mine, which are considered to be recreational, are conducted in the evenings. And Orlock responded to the many gauntlets I'd thrown by not showing up for three nights. I blamed myself for driving him away, but I didn't feel too guilty about it. I just figured that Orlock didn't have any courage when it came to taking risks in his writing.

Then, on a Friday night, he returned. And instead of handing out his customarily vapid ten- to twenty-page string of long words, he distributed a three-page story. Once each of us had a copy in hand, he commenced to read his story out loud. In a quavering voice, with his whole body trembling, Orlock proceeded, through the use of simple, unadorned, and straightforward language, to both entrance and devastate his audience.

The story was about a two-year-old boy who climbs out of his crib one morning. The little boy wanders into his mother's room, where she's sleeping with her boyfriend. The little boy cuddles in bed with them. Then a light bulb goes on in the mom's boyfriend's head, and he suggests that they do something kinky. The mother giggles at the thought and agrees. So that morning they start doing kinky things to the boy—unspeakable kinky things—and pretty soon it becomes a daily ritual.

Orlock was weeping when he finished the story. "Are you satisfied now?" he asked me.

The room was absolutely silent.

"It's a powerful story," I said at last. Then, not knowing what else to say, I praised Orlock for employing admirable restraint, for using an understated voice. I noted that by giving his readers the facts without condemning the antagonists in his story, he avoided the very seductive trap of *telling* his readers what to feel. Had he done so, I said, he would have deflated the tension, thereby undermining the piercing, desolate, and chilling effect he had worked so hard to achieve. He gave us room to emotionally breathe, I told the class, to generate our own sense of outrage. "In the presence of hot emotional subject matter," I said, as I'd said in countless classrooms before, "the use of a cool and understated voice is invariably the most effective strategy."

My literary analysis was on the money. But my words sounded hollow to me. This was a breakthrough moment in Orlock's fucked life—in his fucked-up-beyond-repair of a fucked life—and now it was I, not he, who was hiding behind a mask, in this case the mask of pedagogy. I felt like a hypocrite and rightfully so. I didn't know what to do.

I looked at the other students in the class, but I expected no help from them. Orlock was, after all, a known Baby Raper, and merely to talk to a known Baby Raper, let alone to show sympathy for him, can lead to serious repercussions in prison.

So that's why I assumed the other students in class, most of whom had committed (or at least pretended to have committed) "honorable" crimes such as murder, wouldn't help me get out of this mess; a mess that I, alone, had created by goading Orlock to muck with his demons.

But my assumption proved to be wrong. I had underestimated the decency of my students. They knew, as I did, that the last thing Orlock needed was a technical analysis of his story. And they knew, as I did not, what he needed: to hear that what had happened was not his fault, and that he had, with regard to the horrors he'd endured, absolutely no cause for shame. And so, one by one, slowly and gently, the other students began (I don't know how else to say it) to *coo* to the class pariah. They spoke, in hushed tones, about the terrible things that they, too, had endured when they were children. They told Orlock it must've been rough. They praised him for the courage it took to write his story, and they told him how powerful it was. They quietly talked about the harshness of life, and told Orlock how sorry they were.

We had five or six other submissions to workshop that night, but we didn't get to a single one. Something much bigger and more important was taking place, and it lasted until class was dismissed.

During the course of my residency at Pine Lodge, I had befriended a young administrator. On my last day I dropped by his office to say goodbye. As we reviewed the past two weeks, I asked him where Orlock had been previously incarcerated. My acquaintance made a quick phone call and reported back that Orlock had served a long stretch at Walla Walla (I forget exactly how many years) and that he was due to be released from Pine Lodge in several months.

I imagined that Orlock, a transparent Baby Raper, had led a horrible life at Walla Walla. And I voiced my opinion that Orlock was beyond redemption; that he was, as I read him, a pedophile to the core who was absolutely bound to re-offend.

The young administrator rocked back in his chair, sighed, and then he said that he agreed.

This happened in 1990. I hope and pray that once he was back on the streets, Orlock didn't get a chance to hurt more than one or two children. I hope and pray that he was quickly apprehended, and that he was tried, convicted, and locked up in prison for the rest of his miserable life.

Yet Orlock's crimes, as abhorrent as they are, don't negate the holy nature of that surreal interlude, one Friday night in June, when Orlock said, in effect, "This is who I am. These are the atrocities that were perpetrated against me, and these (albeit through unspoken inference) are the atrocities that I have perpetrated against others." And then, in response to this sordid confession, he received unconditional love.

This was, quite possibly, the only time that Orlock had experienced such pure acceptance, and it is unlikely that he will experience it again. Moreover, in almost a decade of prison teaching, this was the only time I saw the barriers break down; saw the invariably inviolate prison pecking order give way to unrestrained compassion.

■ ■ ■

"I'VE NEVER WRITTEN a story before," Jon Fleming said.

"Then I guess it's time to try one," I said.

The next morning Fleming showed up in class with this:

And I Laughed

Amy was the best dog a boy could own, and she was mine. She came to me as a puppy, a gift for my fifth birthday, a white German shepherd.

We had just moved to Ferndale on Harksell Road. There were fields and woods, joy to a boy and his dog. For three years our friendship grew, as did Amy. I would be late for dinner and Mom would tell her, "Go find Jon," and she would.

We would go camping and she would run all over, coming back to camp wet and muddy, a grin on her face. A happy dog, a happy boy.

One day I let Amy outside. I was eight years old. She ran all over the yard, then across the street to the dairy farm. Rocky, the dairy farmer's son, had gotten a gun for Christmas.

I heard a pop, pop, pop, and saw Amy dancing, jumping into the air. And I laughed. Oh, what a funny dog.

Mom sent me to my room but I looked out my window. Pop, pop, pop. Mom was screaming, "No, stop!"

Amy crawled into our yard. Her legs were red.

Mom called Grandpa. He came over fast. Amy had crawled to the porch. I could hear her yelping. Grandpa lifted his shotgun out of his truck and walked over to Amy. Boom.

We called the sheriff but when they came they did nothing. They said Amy had been chasing cows. The farmers said this, they did. I ran out of my room and told them, "They lie!" but Mother sent me back to my room.

We buried Amy in the back yard, under the plastic pool. I never owned another dog again, and we moved out of the country into Bellingham.

I prayed sometimes that Amy hadn't heard me laugh. What an evil little boy am I.

■ ■ ■

THE WORD "FELL" IS AN IMPORTANT jailhouse term. I have rarely spent a day in prison without hearing at least one student allude to the time before he fell; to the state or county in which he fell; or even to the relief he felt when he finally fell, which is to say the relief he felt when the authorities intervened and ended his criminal career for him.

When those of us who teach in prison speak, write, or even think about our students, we are, of course, dealing with the visibly fallen. That is why it is so easy and commonplace for outsiders to criticize us for expressing compassion for our students, and to assert, wrongly, that we condone their violent actions or that we lack compassion for their victims.

As teachers and as writers, this notion of the fallen poses a dilemma. How do we wend our way through this moral obstacle course—prison—where we frequently witness brutality and injustice being visited upon armed robbers, rapists, murderers, and other convicted sinners?

Perhaps this passage from a speech delivered by Israeli novelist Amos Oz provides an answer:

> Whenever I find that I agree with myself 100 percent, I don't write a story; I write an angry article telling my government what to do (not that it listens.) But if I find more than just one argument in me, more than just one voice, it sometimes happens that the different voices develop into characters and then I know I am pregnant with story. I write stories precisely when I can step into several antagonistic claims, diverse moral stances, conflicting emotional positions. There is an old Hasidic tale about a rabbi who is called upon to judge two conflicting claims to the same goat. He decrees that both claimants are right. Later, at home, his wife says this is impossible: how can both be right when they claim the same goat? The rabbi reflects for a moment and says, "You know, dear wife, you are right, too." Well, sometimes I am that rabbi.
>
> In the end, you pick up your pen and start writing, working like an old-fashioned watchmaker, with a magnifying glass in your eye and a pair of tweezers between your fingers; holding and

inspecting an adjective against the light, changing a faulty adverb, tightening a loose verb, reshaping a worn-out idiom. This is the time when what you are feeling inside you is far from political righteousness. Rather it is a strange blend of rage and compassion, of intimacy with your characters mingled with utter detachment. Like icy fire. And you write. You write not as someone struggling for peace but more like someone who begets peace and feels eager to share it with the readers; *and you write with a single ethical imperative: Try to understand. Forgive some. And forget nothing.*

■ ■ ■

"I STOLE A LOT of cars," a student admitted one day in class. "But at least I didn't steal them from people."

"Then who'd you steal them from?" another student asked.

"From parking lots," the car thief replied.

■ ■ ■

I SPENT SOME TIME TEACHING down in Chehalis, at a maximum security facility called "The Green Hill School." According to the bureaucrats in Olympia, Green Hill was a "juvenile detention facility," but all I ever heard it referred to, by inmates and most staff members alike, was as a "gladiator school." By this they meant that Green Hill served as a training ground for the adult prisons to which, according to demoralizing study after demoralizing study, 80 to 90 percent of Green Hill's graduates would matriculate shortly after their release.

Located in the lush, green dairy farmland of southwestern Washington, Green Hill housed the state's most violent seventeen- to twenty-one-year-old felons. Among the students I had were two murderers who, at the age of seventeen or eighteen, were in for life without parole. For reasons that neither I nor the other teachers understood, by far the less volatile of the two was forced to negotiate his way to and from class wearing leg shackles.

Sometimes, at night, in my Super 8 Motel room, I'd try to figure out how this dignified young man kept going. He was half Cheyenne and half white. He wrote very restrained and eloquent stories about growing up on a ranch, a ranch he would never see again. He had loved to work on that ranch. He was particularly attached to his horse.

I couldn't imagine a sentence of life without parole, especially if I was seventeen. Sooner or later, I reasoned, the young man's childhood memories would become more like dreams than reality. And later still, with the exception of a snippet here and there, he'd lose hold of his childhood completely. All his memories, all his reference points, would be prison. And that would probably make him crazy if he wasn't crazy already. It certainly made *me* a little crazy just to think about that, so I'd try to drop the subject and go to sleep.

When I taught at Green Hill I found that its high concentration of adolescent energy—untempered by the wisdom, regrets, health problems, and other hints of mortality possessed by middle-aged convicts—made this prison for the state's most violent seventeen to twenty-one year olds feel *more* not *less* dangerous than even the most hardcore of Washington's adult prisons. Consequently, when I look back on my teaching career, it hardly strikes me as coincidental that the only time I was physically attacked by an inmate occurred at The Green Hill School.

My assailant—perhaps a crack baby, perhaps a fetal alcohol baby—had frenzied, demonic eyes. I was afraid of those eyes. They were *loco*. They were feral, untamable, and included no hint that the kid who possessed them had ever taken a course in "victim empathy awareness." (And if he had taken and passed the course, you better believe it was a social promotion.)

Since I had absolutely no desire to mix it up with this authentic sociopath who also happened to be big, young, and, I assumed, fast, I developed a strategy: no eye contact. And for three weeks my strategy worked. I handed him papers, I listened to his diatribes, I thanked him for his inane comments during class discussion without once looking up from the floor. But then, one morning, I got sloppy. My glance strayed and I got trapped in a stare. It only lasted an instant (although it felt like forever) and the physical assault commenced immediately. I froze in place, terrified, while the kid threw punches at a very rapid pace. He hit me but didn't inflict nearly as much damage as my utter passivity invited him to. Perhaps he had no desire to spend more time in the hole than was absolutely necessary. Perhaps the kid was more capable of rational thought than I'd previously given him credit for.

In any event, within seconds, three security guards were on him. They had him pinned to the ground in no time flat.

When all was said and done that day, every other student in the class—there were fifteen of them, as I recall—had personally shaken my hand and apologized to me for the behavior of one of their own.

I hardly ever think about the fight. But I'm haunted by the image of those handshakes. The students who came up to me were under no obligation to do so. The apologies didn't earn them a reprieve from harsh treatment, nor did it shorten their stays in prison. So why did they put in the effort to console me when they could just as well have laughed at me for losing the fight and for literally quaking in its aftermath? Why were these violent, dangerous adolescents so exquisitely sensitive to my emotional needs? What possessed them to behave like (and in the process to become) angels, pure and simple, fucking angels?

Based upon many stories I heard while teaching at The Green Hill School, that prison for juveniles lacked nothing, in the way of brutality and injustice, that was handed out to my adult students. In fact, in one punitive arena, at least, the juveniles had it worse.

I am referring to solitary confinement, *a.k.a.*, "the hole." It appears that both Green Hill and its maximum security counterpart for slightly younger juveniles—The Maple Lane School just up the road—handle this matter in a manner that is considerably more cruel than is the case in most modern adult prisons. A little architectural background may be in order: In prisons constructed nowadays, "the hole" is not really a "hole." It's a series of isolation cells, sure, but not like the holes depicted in old movies. Most contemporary isolation cells have a bed, a light, running water, a desk, a few books, letter-writing paper, and so forth. I'm not saying that isolation is a walk in the park. But it's a far cry from the sweltering outhouse of a hole depicted in the movie "Cool Hand Luke."

This is not the case, or so my students claimed, for the young gladiators at Green Hill and Maple Lane. When a juvenile at one of these institutions is sent to "the hole," it really is a "hole"—a pitch dark, malodorous, wooden cell that comes, or so my students insisted, replete with a slop bucket for human waste.

I did not know whether to believe them.

One blazing hot July afternoon at The Maple Lane School—on a pretext of handing out an assignment, although my real motivation was fact-finding—I got permission to visit a student of mine who'd been sent to the hole for raping another inmate. Upon my arrival at the isolation unit, my mind was brimming with questions, and that slop bucket I'd heard so much about was at the top of the list. But my intense curiosity notwithstanding, good breeding, I suppose, or maybe tact (or maybe cowardice) prevented me from asking my student if he really lacked modern plumbing in his cell and if he was, consequently, forced to revert to nineteenth century customs. Nevertheless, merely by slowing time down and standing, surveying, and sniffing, I discovered that much of what I'd heard was true. The cluster of solitary confinement holes at Maple Lane comprised two short and very crowded rows of remarkably narrow and noisome wooden cells, bunched next to each other like some turn-of-the-century Lower East Side tenement built expressly for immigrant midgets. The cells must have been blistering in the ninety-plus degree heat.

My student and I spoke through a tiny wooden slot in his door. As I stood there, taking in the ambiance, I remember feeling peeved. This student was one of the best writers I had. My prison instincts told me that the crime he was incarcerated for was an honorable one, such as killing a man with a knife instead of a gun, or maybe even with his bare hands. For the other students not only respected him, many of them appeared to hold him in awe. Hence, I'd relied heavily on this prized student to maintain class order, to make incisive points during workshop discussions, and to help me tutor other, less experienced writers. But now, by giving into his less savory urges—by raping, or so I imagined it, some poor defenseless, scrawny kid, quite possibly a terrified fresh fish, perhaps, or maybe (to increase his stature) a known and widely disliked rapo—my star student had gotten himself sent to the hole, thereby making my job harder, considerably harder than it had been a few days before.

As I caught myself thinking these unforgivably petty thoughts, I felt a stab of self-loathing. I hated myself, I hated my student, and I hated that disgrace of a hole most of all. "Michael, I gotta go," I said abruptly.

He grunted "good-bye" and closed the slot.

That night I did something I'd never done before, but have done several times subsequently. As a low-cost alternative to five years of potentially fruitless $90-an-hour psychotherapy for post traumatic stress disorder, I can't recommend the technique highly enough: I dealt with my various psychological prison "issues" by driving to a nearby casino and getting utterly, shamelessly plastered.

I was teaching at The Green Hill School on October 3, 1995. That morning, the O.J. Simpson murder trial ended. The jury pronounced O.J. innocent.

As news of O.J.'s acquittal spread throughout the Education Building, I witnessed a phenomenon I'd never seen in prison: contagious glee. There was clapping. There was cheering. Guys were high-fiving and hugging one another. And it wasn't just the black guys who were doing this. It was white guys, Hispanic guys, and Indian guys, too.

I'd been teaching in prisons for a long time by then, long enough to know that white guys, black guys, Hispanic guys, and Indian guys almost always sat at separate tables in the chow hall; long enough to know that it was *de rigeur* for white guys and black guys to hate one another or, in order to survive, to *pretend*, when the occasion called for it (and there was never any shortage of such occasions), that they hated one another. Consequently, no white guy would hoot and holler at the news that O.J. Simpson had been acquitted. No white guy would be *caught dead* rooting for O.J. To do so would be tantamount to an act of racial treason, a very serious breach of jailhouse decorum, such a serious violation of The Convict Code, in fact, that it could well invite a white supremacist type to sink a shank into the perpetrator's back. If I knew nothing about prisons after all my years inside, at least I knew this much: *no white guy would cheer for O.J.*

Or so I had assumed. But obviously, I was wrong. Obviously, my logic was flawed. Or if my logic wasn't exactly flawed, it had at the very least, regressed. Yes, I was thinking like a rookie, like fresh meat.

You see, logic, as you and I know it on "the outs," doesn't work the same way in prison. Our concept of logic doesn't even come close to working the same way as it does in these self-contained far places of the mind; in these eerie funhouse mirrors of the American soul. (That's another thing I'd learned from prison: at the extremes, expect only surprises.)

And this surprise left me utterly flummoxed. No matter how hard I tried to puzzle it out, I couldn't come up with the answer. So once all the victory hoopla ceased, I asked my students to educate me; to please fill me in on the euphoric response that the innocent verdict had unleashed.

Since I lacked the temerity to frame the question in the bold and ugly racial terms that only a prison teacher with a Kamikaze mindset would attempt to tackle head on, I framed my question in the less inflammatory (if equally valid) rhetoric of economic injustice. "I just don't get it," I told the class. Then I went on to explain my confusion. I said regardless of whether he was black or white, the only reason that O.J. got off was that he had millions to spend on his defense. Being rich in the everyday sense of the word wasn't nearly enough, I said. Only an incredibly, *filthy* rich man could hire an entire team of lawyers. And that wasn't all O.J. paid for. His hotshot lawyers, I said, made liberal use of professional evidence experts, the best experts money could buy. These world-renowned authorities on this or that subject earned thousands a day, I said. But curiously, they weren't great scientists. Oh, they had their science down, but what made them so crucial to O.J.'s defense was that they knew how to dazzle a jury. They had impeccable timing, I said. They knew just how and when to trot out their weapons: flip charts, snake oil, smoke, mirrors, and even truth, all of which worked in a synergistic fashion to make monkeys of the L.A. Police Department.

"If any of you had O.J.'s dough, you'd be free men today," I said. "So why don't you resent him? Why aren't you jealous? Why don't you *hate* the guy?"

I looked at my class, a cross-section of poor America, a very poignant and beautiful collection, I thought, of whites, blacks, tans, browns, and various shades of mocha. Not one of my students could afford to hire a first-rate criminal attorney, let alone, like O.J., a whole team of attorneys; of big-name, big-ego, crackerjack lawyers who would make it their business to poke huge holes in what appeared to me, and to millions of other Americans (albeit most of us white) to be an airtight case of guilt.

If one extrapolates inversely—from O.J. to my students—it's pretty easy to understand what money, when *not* spent lavishly, will achieve for a defendant in a court of law. And if one chooses to follow that cynical line of reasoning, then it wasn't the crimes my students committed that brought about their convictions. Rather, it was indigence, simple indigence. Or, to stand the cliché on its head, it *is* a crime to be poor.

So why, I wondered, did O.J.'s acquittal elicit such a joyful response? Why weren't my students angry and sad, profoundly sad, like I was?

Fortunately, I was on pretty good terms with the black students in my class. Otherwise, I could never have gotten away with my "question," which was, of course, no question at all but merely a hodgepodge of very white thoughts (not many of them original) about O.J.

Some of my black students—but only a few—said simply that O.J. was innocent. "Motherfuckers framed him," said one. "Motherfuckers framed him."

And as for the rest of my students? They looked at the floor, they looked at the walls, they looked anywhere in the room but at me.

I knew what my students were thinking. I could *feel* it, and it didn't feel good. "Dumb white privileged Harvard motherfucker," was in the air. It was most definitely in the air that day. "He's too white and too Harvard to ever get it."

And maybe my students were right. Maybe I *would* never get it. And no doubt a tactically smarter teacher would have let the matter drop then and there. He would have acted as if it were no big deal, as if it made no difference to him. By so doing, such a teacher could resume his classroom role, could be the boss-man in charge once again.

But I'm not that kind of teacher. When I have to know something, *I just have to know,* even if my dignity takes a beating. "Won't someone enlighten me, please?" I implored. "Just give me the answer and I'll shut up."

More staring at the walls ensued. Some of the guys were finding their fingernails to be objects of great fascination. Then, finally, *finally,* Raymond stirred. Raymond, a Lummi Indian from way up north—just a short drive from the Canadian border—was a story-writing teacher's dream. He had a flair both for writing and for feeding my ego because he loved to soak up knowledge about the craft.

"O.J. beat The Man," Raymond quietly said. "He beat The Man, Robert. Don't you see?"

Raymond's utterance broke the tension in the room. In no time at all guys were laughing again, high-fiving each other, and hugging. "O.J. kicked some ass! He beat The Man!"

As for me, I just sat there and considered the implications of Raymond's strong, quiet words. I looked at my students blowing off steam, and suddenly, as if our brains were intertwined, their thoughts became apparent to me. My students were focused, for a giddy few minutes, not on a sensational double murder in L.A. (murders, and the gore that accompanies them, don't exactly make for big news in prison), but rather on the concept of Justice. Or, more precisely, on the American System of Justice, and what a bitter, bitter joke it is to defendants, like themselves, who have no money.

O.J., however, was different. O.J. was rolling in dough. And he'd used up his dough to pull a fast one on the country. Hell, he'd pulled a fast one on the world! And my oh my, but it was *slick*.

He'd used trickery, chicanery, and above all, lots of jack—The Rich White Man's Approach, in short—to beat The Rich Man at The Rich Man's own game. Moreover (and this is the most delicious part), O.J., a black man, had won the game by playing with strict adherence to The White Man's Rules, special rules that had evolved over centuries.

And how and why had these rules evolved? Back at Harvard, they might attempt to answer this question by starting with the *Magna Carta*. And there's much to be said for taking a stroll, and a thorough and leisurely stroll at that, through the evolution of modern Western philosophy, institutions, social history, and political thought. But not just now, if you please. For at Green Hill or Maple Lane or any prison in the land, it is desperation that rules. And when despair is the prevailing state of mind, there is time to consider only those questions that might alleviate suffering in the present.

Or, to put it another way, it is highly unlikely that on any given day, you'll find throngs of convicts standing around, holding impassioned intellectual discussions in the rain-soaked muddy Big Yard, engaged in at-times stormy debates about the passage of power from the few to the many that began with the signing of the *Magna Carta*. (No offense intended to the academic community, and to political scientists specifically, but when you're constantly worried about getting shanked in the back, it's a bit of a challenge to work up an interest in an ancient piece of paper with a screwy name.)

Which is not to say that my students are apathetic. It's just that they are highly focused. They care a great deal about the present and future status of the aforementioned White Man's Rules (from which, it ought to go without saying, white convicts are not exempt). Most of those rules are codified by law, a few by tradition only. But here in America, it is those rules, and no others, that serve the purpose of defending, maintaining, and in some cases oppressing, the legal status of us all. Which is to say, those rules preserve the *status quo*.

It's a powerful force, the *status quo*. But occasionally, even the *status quo* gets knocked on its sorry ass. Not for long, mind you, but it happens. Witness the O.J. verdict. It was a verdict that set what appeared to be a guilty killer free, and the rejoicing that occurred at The Green Hill School—a "school" for the socioeconomically doomed—was intriguing, I admit, to watch.

White and black students were celebrating together, talking, laughing, high-fiving. This rarely happens outside of prison, and never inside. Never.

I looked over at Raymond and he looked back and shrugged. No one would believe what we were seeing.

But today was different, I guess. Today, O.J. Simpson beat The Man.

Hence, the bittersweet (to my mind) hoopla. Hence this unheard of multi-racial display; this ephemeral wave of inclusive good will that swept through the prison, then disappeared.

■ ■ ■

MICHAEL COLLINS MADE the mistake of robbing convenience stores in two states. Consequently, after serving almost six years in Washington, Collins was shipped off to Oregon to do a stint there. He was incarcerated at the Oregon Correctional Institution in Pendleton.

In his letters to me, Collins described Pendleton as a bleak and unhappy place. He said that living conditions were horrendous and that this was reflected by the suicide rate. Between January and July 1994, there were seven suicide attempts, four of which were completely successful, and three of which inflicted serious damage on the participants. In every case, both successful and unsuccessful, the attempts were carried out by one method: jumping off the fourth floor stairwells that served as exits to the living units.

Collins reported that one jumper appeared to have had a change of heart in mid-flight, and tried to glide onto the grass. He was unable to alter his trajectory, however, and landed on concrete and died.

Another convict who jumped and died smashed his head flat in the process. But the guards weren't taking any chances: they handcuffed the corpse and left the cuffs on until a coroner pronounced the corpse dead.

This situation was clearly bad for morale, and it did not reflect favorably on the administration. So after the seventh plunge, the prison administration addressed the situation. They did so by caging off the open parts of the stairwells with an impenetrable wrapping of razor wire. This made it physically impossible to jump, and in this way death by plunging was eradicated.

■ ■ ■

ONE REASON WHY prison sentences in Great Britain are typically shorter than those in the United States is that psychologists have determined that individuals who are incarcerated for ten or more contiguous years tend to become "institutionalized." These individuals are so damaged by their lengthy stays in prison that they cannot successfully reintegrate into the society at large.

Such reliable and potentially useful data notwithstanding, prison sentences in the United States are notoriously long and growing longer. The reason for the promulgation of this counter-productive policy is as simple as it is cynical, and it is particularly apparent during election years. (When was the last time you heard a political candidate promise to *not* "get tough on crime?")

Once a convict becomes institutionalized, the freedom he longs for is also a source of profound fear. I heard lots of stories—from guards and cons alike—about the odd behaviors exhibited by long-term prisoners as their release dates approached. They screamed in their sleep; they became suicidal; they'd suddenly start to commit infractions in order to prolong their stays in the prison womb. I even heard about one lifer who escaped from the Washington State Reformatory in Monroe; established a new identity and a new life (replete with car, wife, job, and house) in California; and then, four years later, literally showed up on the front steps of the Reformatory because he just couldn't hack it out there. I'd never quite trusted the student who told this story, but when I relayed it to an administrator who was always straight with me, he said the story was, indeed, true.

■ ■ ■

. . . *"YOU FUCKING RETARD get out of bed right now! Do you hear me boy? You better get moving you dumb little fuck."*

"Yes, Dad, I am moving. What did I do this time?"

"Take off your clothes you little shit."

I undress slowly. Dad walks out of the room. He shuts the door. In the next room I hear running bathtub water. The sound of water stops.

I look around the room, knowing what will happen next. I hear the bathroom door open and close. My bedroom door flies open. Dad walks into the bedroom. In one hand, the wet razor strap, in the other a rubber hose. He puts the rubber hose down on my bed.

"Get over there next to the chair. You know what to do, retard."

I put my hands on the arm of the sofa chair.

"Put your head down in the seat, retard."

I lower my head into the back part of the chair.

"Get those legs out farther from the chair you dumb shit."

I hear the rushing air of the wet razor strap. The strap stings again and again. I can barely breathe; the pain keeps coming. After a while, the hitting stops.

"Stand up, retard."

I stand up. I look down over my body. The welts and bruises are starting to show. Dad walks back and in his hands is the rubber hose. He swings full force. The hose hits my face with great impact. He lands a second blow across my face, then starts working his way down my body.

"Open your legs, boy. I am going to give you something to remember for the rest of your life."

He steps back. The logging boot comes straight up between my legs. I yell at the top of my lungs. Then things go black from the pain.

I wake up in the cold water of the bathtub.

"Here, drink this, retard." He hands me a bottle of whiskey. "Do you know why this happened to you?"

"No, Dad. Why?"

"The fight you were in yesterday. Fighting over a fucking girl, and losing the fight at that! No losing fights, do you understand? Never lose another fight. Is that clear?"

"Yes, Dad."

"You had everything coming to you, retard..."

from the story "Cindy" by Lesley Smith

...Mr. Brown calls our home that night and tells Barry, my Mom's boy-friend, that we were playing in the quarry that afternoon. Barry comes into the bedroom and takes us into the kitchen. The electric stove is on high. The rings on the stove are red hot. Barry drags me to the stove. He takes both his hands and puts them around one of my hands. He places my hand on the red hot ring of the electric stove. I try real hard to pull away from him, but he's too strong.

Barry takes my other hand and places it on a red hot ring. The pain is so bad that things go black around me...

from the story "Barry" by Lesley Smith

Lesley Smith was a student of mine at the Washington Corrections Center in Shelton. He was serving a twenty-year sentence for attempted murder. Smith was two years younger than I, but owing, I suppose, to the hardness of his life, he looked a good ten years older, maybe more. He had a long gray beard, a head of gray hair, and a kindly if careworn face.

Smith was working on a series of true life stories about his up-bringing in Leavenworth, Washington. As you've no doubt surmised from the preceding excerpts, Smith's life had been no walk in the park. A fellow student suggested, only partly in jest, that once Smith completed his book about his youth, he should entitle it *Surrounded by Assholes.*

One day, after workshopping yet another gruesome story (this one about incest in Smith's family) I asked him how he dealt with all of this. I pointed out that he never sounded angry in his stories. Why wasn't he seething with rage?

Smith shrugged and said the past was the past, and that he'd forgiven all those people long ago.

I looked into his eyes and saw no sign of a lie. He looked peaceful, sad, and resigned.

Then I thought about myself and all the grudges I carried against people who had slighted or mistreated me. These slights were infinitesimal, of course, when compared to what Smith had endured. But I've held onto my anger; I won't let it go. I don't even know *how* to let it go. Consequently, my life is littered with castoffs; with people I haven't spoken to for years. With regard to this matter of forgiveness, it was evident, Lesley Smith was a far better man than I.

It was just the two of us there, alone in the room. All the other students had gone to chow. I could've told Smith what was going through my mind. I could've told him he was better than I. I could've told him his capacity for granting absolution made me painfully aware of my pettiness. But owning up to one's defects is a hard thing to do, and owning up to a convict is even harder. I was, ostensibly, Smith's moral superior, a position I was loathe to relinquish. So I chose to keep my thoughts to myself, and walked out of the classroom to get some lunch.

■ ■ ■

ONE DAY IN CLASS WE were playing a game that I call Stories Spawn Stories. It is based on the premise that we are a story-telling and a story-hearing species. There is no culture that has ever been studied that doesn't have its stories. Story telling and story hearing is intrinsic to us.

Consequently, if I tell you a personal story, you automatically think about a related personal story of your own, and depending upon the way I choose to set up the game, you either tell your story only to me; tell it to the person next to you; or, if, as a class, we have created a safe enough haven in which to tell everyone our personal stories, you tell your story to the entire class.

This exercise is a useful teaching tool. Oral story swapping is a relatively non-threatening way to blur the oft-intimidating line between the oral and the written story, proving to every member of the class, even to those with low writing skills, that they have valid stories to tell by virtue of the fact that they're alive.

Oral story swapping may also be used as a relaxation technique, something a writing class does just for fun. It's a technique for taking a break from the hard work required to analyze written stories, and all the structural problems that attend them. So that's what we were doing one Friday afternoon: we were taking a breather from workshopping written stories by swapping some oral stories.

I started things off by telling the class an absurd and highly embellished account of an incident pertaining to one of the seven dogs I owned when I was growing up. I did my best to set a light, easy tone.

Kurt, who was on my right, went next. And so it proceeded around the room until we came to Glenn.

Glenn was different from most of the guys in class. He was a little older, a little gruffer, and considerably more hardcore. "He's an old-school convict," as my supervisor had put it to me. "He'll 'game' you [prison jargon for 'try to trip you up'] for sure."

Glenn had a broad back, a thick neck, and thick stumpy arms. He wore prison issue faded blue overalls and a railroad engineer's cap.

He also had beady black eyes. I'd read about "beady eyes" all my life, but I'd never actually seen a pair until I encountered Glenn's. They looked like the small, black eyes on the fish on the beds of ice at the seafood counter at the supermarket.

During the first two weeks of this four-week residency, Glenn hadn't turned in any stories, nor had he made any comments during the course of workshop discussion. I assumed he'd pass on this story-swapping exercise as well, but he didn't. Instead, like the rest of us, he told a dog story, a story that was notably terse.

"When I was five years old," he began, "our fucking bitch had a litter of fucking puppies. When the little fuckers were about two weeks old, I tried to make them sit. But they wouldn't sit for me. So I strangled them one by one."

Glenn leaned back and smiled at me, the first time he'd smiled in two weeks. His beady eyes gleamed with malevolence. I didn't wonder *if* but rather *how* he knew that cruelty to animals is the one single crime I absolutely cannot abide.

He said, "How did I do, Mr. Gordon?"

■ ■ ■

DURING ACADEMIC YEAR 1995–96, I spent five weeks teaching story writing at the Clallam Bay Corrections Center. CBCC is the most remote of Washington's prisons, located way out on the tip of the Olympic

Peninsula, just a few miles east of Cape Flattery, the northwestern-most point of the continental United States. Very few people live in this vast, wild territory where rainfall averages 300 inches per year.

Among the state's convict population, CBCC has a sinister repu-tation, even more sinister than that of Washington's other maximum security prison, the Penitentiary at Walla Walla. Movement is so re-stricted at CBCC that the prison verges on a state of permanent lockdown. In almost every respect—geographical, meteorological, and punitive—CBCC represents the final stop, the end of the road, the deepest level of Institutional Hell.

During the time I taught at CBCC, violent offenders (*e.g.* pistol-whipping robbers as opposed, say, to drug dealers) comprised ap-proximately 25 percent of Washington's total prison population. At CBCC, 87 percent of the population was violent, and, a guard told me at a tavern one night, these violent offenders were the worst of the worst, the ones the other prisons couldn't handle. Most of the mur-derers in my class, he said, weren't your everyday run-of-the-mill kill-ers. Rather, he said, they were cold-blooded, remorseless men who'd truly enjoyed their line of work. And the rapists in my class, he said, weren't your commonplace date-rapists. Rather, he said, they were vicious fucking animals. He'd read their jackets, he said. He knew.

"Even Smith?" I said.

Smith was one of my favorites: a slight, soft-spoken, and diligent student who seemed too gentle for this hardcore joint.

The guard sneered at me over his beer. Smith, he said, was a knife-wielding sadist who was heavily into mutilation. Smith sliced off the nipples of his victims.

There was no way to determine if the guard was telling the truth, or if he was merely trying to scare me. If the guard was employed at any other prison, I would have *known* he was talking shit; that he was doing his best to glamorize his job, to make it sound more dangerous than it was. But I'd been around the prison block a few times, and I sensed, in my gut, that CBCC held more than its share of bloody secrets.

For reasons I chose not to inquire about (probably a bureaucratic snafu) one day I received, in my faculty mailbox, a new printout of my class. The printout categorized my students by the crimes they'd committed, and it listed their release dates.

I wish I could say I was utterly appalled by the acts of violence perpetrated by my students; that my first response, upon scanning the printout, was visceral empathy for their victims. I must admit, however, that that was not the case. "Murder I" or "Murder II" were just words on a page, sterile terms devoid of bloodshed and pain; words that didn't so much as begin to convey their tragic, gory stories to me.

What did strike me, however, in a visceral way, were the release dates for my students. A few were due to be freed in the 1990s. But they were the exceptions. Most of the twenty-odd students in my class were slated to be released in the twenty-first century, and of that group, many wouldn't see the light of day until well into the twenty-first century. Or, to put it another way, their youth and middle age would be squandered in prison, and they would either die inside or (conceivably worse) re-acquire their freedom when they were old, unemployable, and utterly forsaken, bereft of family and non-incarcerated friends.

As I pondered the implications of a life sentence at CBCC, I was reminded, once again, of TJ Granack's haunting observation: "I live with hundreds of men pronounced dead on arrival, men who aren't sure if the struggle back to life is possible or even worthwhile." Yet the human spirit is resilient, and there were plenty of convicts at CBCC who didn't succumb to the call of depression or insanity; who tried to make the best of their lousy situations, and to seek what pleasures they could find.

Consequently, I shouldn't have been surprised, one afternoon, when a new student showed up in class. He was a clothes-model thin and very pretty young man who had a smooth and flawless *cafe au lait* complexion. He was dressed in neatly pressed pants and a finely tapered purple shirt, and he wore mascara and black nail polish.

As any fan of HBO prison movies could tell you, this pretty young man didn't own himself. He was clearly a bitch—a sex-slave, a punk—who, in exchange for protection, was somebody's wife, and that someone turned out to be Olson.

Even before he brought his bitch to class, Olson had made an impression on me. He was tall and broad-shouldered, and the tight T-shirts he wore revealed an intimidating set of muscles. Though his stories were in need of vast improvement, the other students were clearly afraid of Olson, and their criticisms were uncharacteristically tentative.

In addition to his bulk, Olson stuck out in my mind because he was the only student I ever had who boasted about his method for committing murders. He was partial, he said, to beheading his victims with a fifteen-inch long bowie knife.

But what really made Olson memorable—made him a student I'll never forget—was his indiscriminate use of semi-colons. Olson's semi-colons materialized, again and again, in absolutely non-existent junctures; in places where nothing *approaching* a pause could in any way whatsoever be justified. He inserted semicolons in lieu of periods and commas. They bisected single-clause sentences. And every so often a semicolon would appear in the midst of a three- or four-word phrase.

During my first couple of weeks at CBCC, I attacked this problem with zeal. In both my typed notes to Olson and in my oral commentary in class, I emphasized the need, the *imperative* need, to employ semicolons judiciously. I pointed out that the capricious use of semi-colons interrupts the narrative flow; that it breaks the all-important fictional artifice, undermines profluence, and so forth. But it was all to no avail. Olson continued to sabotage his sentences by peppering them with semicolons, and, ultimately, I let the matter go.

As for Olson's new seat mate—his sex slave, his wife—well, the pretty young man never turned in an assignment, nor did he participate in class discussion. So what was he doing in the workshop? He was, I supposed, a status symbol of sorts, a jailhouse version of a Rolex watch, a flashy ornament to impress Olson's peers.

Since the Olson I knew would never be a candidate for husband of the year, I pitied the pretty young man. I wondered if he'd been savagely raped by Olson and by numerous other prison bulldogs. I wondered if he'd been purchased for a few packs of cigarettes or sold to settle a gambling debt. I'd heard about prison sex slaves, of course, but this was the first one I'd seen up close, and it really did a number on my head. However, I couldn't afford to spend much time indulging my revulsion and curiosity: I had twenty other students to attend to. And so, with some effort, I stopped dwelling upon the nature of the sex slave's life. I came to regard him (when I regarded him at all) as a pricey but insignificant wrist watch, and I gave no more thought to the daily horrors he endured than I did to those absurd semi-colons.

■ ■ ■

A MURDERER told me this story. He said he'd been in county jail for over a year while he was waiting for his trial to take place. Eventually he lost his case and was sentenced to life in prison. So he was shipped to the state R-Units (Receiving and Processing) at the Washington Corrections Center in Shelton. He said, "I had to take all these psychological tests, and I had to fill out an intake questionnaire. And one of the questions, I swear to God, was 'Are you satisfied with your sex life?'"

■ ■ ■

I<small>T WAS A</small> F<small>RIDAY</small> afternoon in early April, and I was ambling, briefcase full of student stories in hand, from the Education Building toward Main Control at the Washington Corrections Center in Shelton. Once I reached Main Control, I'd trade my staff badge for my car keys, and leave the institution not just for the day but for the weekend.

That morning, I'd checked out of the Super 8 Motel where I'd spent the last five nights, and I was looking forward to a quiet weekend at home, away, for at least two days, from what I sometimes, in my unspoken thoughts, referred to as the Spiritual Emergency Ward. I relished prison teaching almost as much as I relished writing, and no work I have done before or since has made me feel more useful. Still, as previously noted, prison teaching exacts a toll on the psyche. I was glad I was going home.

The Washington Corrections Center at Shelton is spread out like a ranch, and in good weather it's a pleasant walk to the front gate. I could smell the evergreen trees that grew thickly on the hillsides just west of the prison. I could discern a faint sea tang from the nearby Hood Canal. I was walking on concrete, sure, and to my right stood the prison's own prison, the Intensive Management Unit or IMU— The Hole. The two-story IMU, with its deeply recessed narrow slits that passed for windows, was ringed by many rolls of barbed concertina wire. The soft spring air that I was savoring would never reach the IMU's inhabitants, some of whom had lived there, in tiny cells, and in a state of permanent lockdown, for years. If they acted up, or so my students told me, they got maced. If they were raging, or so the cops told me, they threw their own urine and feces at the guards. And some of them, I'd heard, went slowly, quietly (you might even say politely), mad.

I decided it was too nice a day to dwell on the horrors of life in the hole, so I forced myself to look the other way. To my left was a strip of grass leading up to a flower garden that bordered the prison infirmary. I saw two convicts, both young and white, digging a ditch by the garden. They were taking their time, standing shirtless in the sun, soaking up the rays. I heard bits of conversation, and I soon became aware that the subject of discussion was me. "No, I *know* him," one of the two guys was saying to the other. "I had him at Greenhill. Dude's okay."

Green Hill is the state's maximum security prison for juvenile offenders. Evidently, my defender was a former juvenile student who had graduated to adult prison.

"Hey teacher!" he yelled. "How ya doin'?"

"Fine," I said. "Just fine."

"Going home?" my former student asked.

"For the weekend," I said. "I'll be back."

I started to walk again.

"Hey teacher!" my former student yelled.

I stopped walking and put my heavy briefcase down.

"Did the Holocaust really happen?"

My lighthearted mood vanished instantly. I knew what this question meant. It meant that these two young and quite possibly gullible convicts were being recruited by the members of some white supremacist gang. And now, thanks to the state legislature, the recruiters stood a good chance of success. For Washington's prison education program—the Department of Corrections' best hedge against ignorance—was, by legislative fiat, in the process of being dismantled. (Indeed, though I didn't know it at the time, I was mid-way through my final prison teaching stint.)

However, it wasn't my job security that concerned me just then. Rather, I was worried because, as matters now stood, ignorance could and would run rampant throughout the prison, unchecked by any pocket of resistance. Hatred, based on odious lies, would flourish in the absence of education.

"Yes," I said. "It happened."

"I heard that it didn't," said my former student.

"Trust me," I said. "It happened."

"Six million Jews?"

"Plus Gypsies," I said. "Six million plus Gypsies and homosexuals."

"See?" said my former student as he turned to his friend.

"Maybe he's lying," said the friend.

My former student looked over at me. "No shit?" he said.

"No shit."

"Well, I heard it never happened," he said again.

I shrugged, picked up my briefcase, and made a bee line for Main Control.

■ ■ ■

IN OCTOBER 1993, I published a novel entitled *When Bobby Kennedy Was a Moving Man*. In the preface to the novel, it is established that the Celestial Judges can't decide if Bobby's good public works outweighed his private sins. They don't know whether they should admit him to Heaven or send him to Hell. Finally, after twenty years of legal wrangling, the Judges throw up their hands and send Bobby, as a forty-two year old adult, back to earth. The Judges want to see how Bobby behaves the second time around.

Bobby is provided with full memory of his past, along with some magical powers. These powers enable him to perform many wonderful marvels. He is capable, for example, of levitating heavy oak dressers to help his fellow moving men. However, Bobby is proscribed from using his magical powers to influence elections on behalf of liberal Democrats; to exact revenge on his former political opponent, that pissant, Eugene McCarthy; or for monetary or other forms of personal gain. If Bobby abuses his powers, he will lose them.

Since Bobby is a Kennedy male, it should come as no surprise to learn that he abuses his powers in an attempt to seduce a beautiful young woman. The Celestial Judges make good on their threat, and Bobby is swiftly deprived of his magical powers. He becomes a mere mortal who cannot levitate so much as a pencil, let alone a heavy oak dresser.

The loss of his magical powers upsets Bobby so much that his once exemplary performance at work takes a precipitous nose dive. He gets fired, goes temporarily insane, and commits a crime: he attempts to rub out Carlos Marcello, the Mafia Boss who ordered the assassination of Jack. Bobby's plan is well-laid, but at the last minute his gun jams. He is arrested, tried, convicted of first degree attempted murder, and sentenced to life in prison.

Shortly after Bobby starts to serve his sentence, he is subjected to a digital rape. The scene begins when a sadistic guard named Gerbil orders Bobby to be shackled hand and foot. Gerbil and two other guards drag Bobby into a cold concrete room. Bobby is forced to lean over a table while the guards pull his pants and underpants down. Gerbil inserts a finger into Bobby's rectum (a procedure which, in jailhouse jargon, is known as a "finger wave"). Gerbil rubs his finger up and down. He also rubs his groin up against Bobby: he is sexually aroused. As he continues to waggle his finger, Gerbil wonders aloud if a bump he is feeling inside Bobby's asshole is contraband, a hemorrhoid, or just a stray piece of shit. The other guards laugh appreciatively. Then Gerbil makes an odd remark: he says he's disappointed that he doesn't have to work on Christmas. Since all guards get paid triple-time on Christmas whether they work or not, one of his cohorts asks Gerbil, "Why?"

Gerbil responds by saying that he will miss the opportunity to sass the convicts for being in prison on Christmas Day.

I am pleased to say that most of my prison students and most of my fellow moving men told me they liked the book. However, a number of my upper-class, well-educated, and non-incarcerated friends told me that they'd found the book in general and the rape scene in particular very hard to take. And of those upper-class readers, one couple I knew went a step further: they said that the mere fact that I could *conceive* of such a perverse scene suggested that I had some "issues" to work out, and (they were only trying to help, they assured me) I should consider seeing a therapist.

Although I did my best to nod gravely and strike a thoughtful pose when I received this heartfelt advice, I didn't, in fact, take it seriously. After all, the digital rape scene wasn't my idea: I'd simply purloined it from one of my students.

He'd told the story during smoke break one day. He said the finger wave took place back when he was incarcerated at the State Penitentiary in Walla Walla. According to the student, the guard really did joke aloud about what he was feeling inside the student's asshole, and the guard really did express regret about not working on Christmas. The only item I invented was the bit about Gerbil's arousal.

But getting back to the student: when I expressed my horror about what he'd endured, the student shrugged and said there was nothing unusual about it, that these pointless violations occurred all the time. He went on to explain that according to the guards, the impromptu finger waves were conducted to search for contraband. In view of the fact that the guards never bothered to pat down their victims, however, the contraband excuse was flimsy.

As was frequently the case throughout my prison teaching career, I didn't know what to believe. So after class was over that day I asked my supervisor, who used to work at Walla Walla, if the story I'd heard was true. My supervisor said he couldn't vouch for that particular student because he hadn't known him at Walla Walla. However, my supervisor told me the student was, broadly speaking, correct: body cavity searches that were unaccompanied by pat searches had indeed been carried out routinely at Walla Walla during the early 1980s.

"I don't get it," I said. "What's in it for the cops? I'd hate to give a finger wave to anyone."

My supervisor sighed, as he tended to do, whenever I asked a foolish question; a question, that is, to which the obvious answer was staring me right in the face. "Go home and think about it," he said.

It took a night's sleep to figure it out but the next day, when I woke up, I had the answer. The reason the guards liked to rape shackled convicts is that they enjoyed wielding absolute power. They enjoyed it immensely, in fact. It's one of the perks of working in prisons, this opportunity to wield unchecked power; inordinate, unchecked, out of control fucking power.

Fucking power, I thought. How obvious. The insight played in my head like some warped prison mantra: *fucking power, fucking power, fucking power.*

■ ■ ■

LITTLE TONY WAS the tiniest and youngest looking convict student I ever taught. Yet his size and age notwithstanding, I saw no sign that Little Tony had reason to live in fear of sexual enslavement. On the contrary. He was treated with respect by the other convicts in class, all of whom appeared to be older and were certainly much bigger. Moreover, another student told me, Little Tony was down for life without parole. Consequently, I presumed that Little Tony's crime was a very honorable one, most likely a multiple murder.

This was at the old McNeil Island Corrections Center, that filthy, drafty monster of an institution where, as noted earlier in this book, eight men and one toilet inhabited barred, open-tiered cells that were considerably smaller than the average household's living room.

Given these horrifying living conditions, any convict who lived in a one-man cell was considered to be lucky. But there was, as you might expect, a catch: in order to qualify for a solo cell, it had to be determined, by the prison authorities, that the convict in question was insane.

I never did find out the precise nature of Little Tony's diagnosis. All I knew was that he qualified for a one man-cell, and that, as Little Tony explained it, he had several imaginary friends. He hardly ever slept, he said, because he spent most of his nights talking to his imaginary friends. I remember that one of them was named "Shadowfax." I forget the names of the others.

I first heard about Little Tony's imaginary friends one morning during break. About half of the class was outside smoking in the raw February rain. The remaining students, Little Tony among them, were lounging in the prison library where the writing workshop was being held.

As Little Tony talked about his nighttime companions in a matter of fact tone of voice, some of the other students backed him up. Yes, they assured me, Little Tony really did converse all night with his imaginary friends. No, this wasn't bullshit: this was the truth.

The convicts were talking about Little Tony's insanity as if it were nothing more remarkable than the weather, and this seemed strange to me. Why were the convicts so cavalier? Why didn't they regard Little Tony's state of mind to be tragic, alarming, and abnormal?

That night, at the Motel 6 where I was staying, I thought the matter over. And I came to understand that Little Tony's fellow convicts were right. There really *wasn't* anything remarkable about Little Tony's affliction, at least not once you considered his situation. He lived in a hideous place, a veritable modern-day dungeon. And his youth notwithstanding, he was down for life without parole. He was doomed to spend decade upon decade, in short, living, without hope, in Hell.

Under the circumstances, Little Tony's particular variety of insanity was not only a coping mechanism: it was, quite possibly, a *healthy* coping mechanism. And healthy or not, it is self-evident that Little Tony's imaginary friends provided far more in the way of love, acceptance, affection, and comfort than prison ever could.

For several months after my residency, I prayed every night for Little Tony. I beseeched whoever is in charge of our souls to permit Little Tony to keep his imaginary friends. "It would be unwise to let him go sane," I'd point out. "Please let him stay crazy," I'd implore.

My supplications, though unconventional, were fitting. For it was, in the twisted context of prison, clearly and indisputably in Little Tony's best interests to maintain his present level of derangement.

Postlude
Love in the Prison Classroom

This address was delivered by Robert Ellis Gordon to Department of Corrections administrators and teachers on September 16, 1993.

FOR THOSE OF YOU WHO DON'T know me, my name is Robert Gordon and I've taught story writing in the prisons since 1989. Some years I've taught only one two-week residency. Other years I've spent as much as four months teaching inside.

Today, I'd like to address two questions:

1. What, if we're doing our best, can we hope to accomplish in a prison classroom, and;

2. What, beyond imparting knowledge about our art form, are the stakes we're really playing for?

I'd like to begin by talking about the subject of love in the prison classroom, on the subject of loving our students. I am not, of course, referring to romantic or sexual love, but to what would normally be deemed to be appropriate love (call it caring if you will), to the way in which any good, committed teacher handles his or her charges.

Some students respond best to what is commonly referred to as tough love. Others—the most abused, whipped puppies in class—deserve respectful, distant love. Some require nothing more than gentle love—the quiet love that enables them to give themselves permission to write their true and oft-wrenching stories. And some students, frequently the hardest and most interesting cases, test us by demanding copious amounts of patient love.

Any competent teacher who has taught in the brutal prison environment could tell you about the transformative power of love—to the tiny and not-so-tiny miracles that occur every day; miracles that occur at a far more rapid rate than in a standard school or university classroom.

I, myself, could probably tell you a hundred such stories. But don't worry, I will only tell you one. It's about a student I had at the McNeil Island Corrections Center several years ago. He was a very magnetic and intelligent man. He was also a disciple of Louis Farrakhan, and a very militant disciple at that. He frequently expressed the belief that a race war in America was inevitable. (He'd been convicted, in fact, of running guns.) And he intimated, on more than one occasion, that certain white people—by virtue of their right-wing political beliefs or their religious affiliation—should be rounded up and summarily killed. All of which is to say, this student was steeped in dogma. Consequently, the stories he wrote for the class were considerably less satisfactory than they might have been.

That is one price people pay when they don the protective mask of dogma. It doesn't make any difference if the dogma is religious or political, or if it comes from the left or the right. Dogma is dogma and when the writer sees the world in simple, rigid, and absolute terms, characters become cardboard figures; empathy is absent; and moralizing takes the place of artful, inviting storytelling.

One day this student, this very militant disciple of Louis Farrakhan, discovered that I was Jewish. And this posed a problem for him.

The problem was not that he disliked or lacked respect for me. The problem was just the opposite: we had a good rapport. And there was no way that he could hold these contradictory truths: the fact, on the one hand, that he liked me, and the fact, on the other hand, that according to the tenets of his political religion, I was supposed to be a professional oppressor; a greedy, loudmouthed, large-nosed, and independently wealthy candidate for ethnic cleansing: one who deserved to be killed.

All of which is not to imply that I'm flawless. I have more than my share of flaws. But I wasn't in class to oppress this student, and as all my close friends can attest, the question of independent wealth is moot because I've never been independently solvent.

But to get back to this student: he was exasperating. Which is to say he demanded patient love. Lots and lots of patient love. You see, he found it necessary to come at me again and again, found it necessary to prove that I was the devil I wasn't in order to hold onto the belief system that had sustained him for so long.

So he came at me. And did not achieve his goal. And in the process of failing to turn me into something and someone I wasn't, this student began to soften. By the end of the fiction workshop, a few stories had emerged; bittersweet stories about the projects where he grew up; stories he invariably sabotaged at the end with clunky and self-evident moralizing. But at least he was making some progress.

I left and he moved on to another teacher—a composition teacher—a woman who was very patient, very loving, and, much to the dismay of this student, also Jewish. He had done everything he could to get in my face, and now, due to the vagaries of academic scheduling, we were all over his.

Over the next couple of years, I followed his literary efforts from a distance. And in time, under the patient tutelage of his new teacher, the mask of dogma disintegrated. Stories emerged; touching, angry, artful, and genuine stories emerged, indeed erupted. This student was allowing himself to experience pain, to experience direct, unfiltered emotion. And the work he produced was first rate.

Now I can't tell you with certainty that when this man hits the streets he will never pose a danger to others; that he will never hurt another human being again. No one can say that about any violent convict with certainty, and you should beware of those who do. Consider, for example, the tragedy that ensued when Norman Mailer lobbied successfully for the release of the convict-author, Jack Henry Abbott. Abbott was a brilliant writer, to be sure, but he was also unstable and explosive. And so, shortly after achieving his freedom, Abbott stabbed a man to death.

That cautionary tale aside, however, I *can* tell you, with a fair amount of certainty, that at this moment in time, my former student, the militant disciple of Louis Farrakhan and the most vicious anti-Semite I've ever known, is less dangerous than he was a few years ago. Because he experienced love at the hands of two teachers who happened to be Jewish, it would be impossible for him to kill us—as might once have been possible—in a relatively sterile fashion. He knows we have faces, he knows we have souls, he knows we are every bit as human as he is. And though our lives have been less tragic and less violent and more privileged than his, we have become far too human for him to murder without empathy.

Over the years, I have given a great deal of thought to those two questions I mentioned earlier: what can we hope to accomplish inside, and what are the true stakes we're playing for? And I have come to realize that in every prison classroom in which I've taught—in every prison classroom that any of us teach—there is a continuum from the least to the most redeemable convict student.

At the top of this continuum—if you are lucky—you will find one student, maybe two, who emanate, for lack of a better word, the quality that we call grace. Make no mistake: these are people who have committed serious, oft-heinous crimes. They have, quite possibly, destroyed lives. They have invariably hit bottom, a very deep bottom, the likes of which you and I have never known. And they have managed, God knows how, to emerge from the spiritual undermuck; to accept full responsibility for their crimes, and to emerge, on the other side, healed.

There are times when a prison classroom is electric with tension and unspoken pain. If you are lucky enough to have one or two of these students who emanate grace, look over in their direction. They will, through a simple smile or nod, enable you to continue with your job.

At the other end of the spectrum you will find the least redeemable students in class. These individuals are raging inside. They are often palpably twisted. They are almost always excellent students. But fiercely devoted as I am to my students as students (and my reputation as a bleeding heart notwithstanding), I am both frightened and saddened by the prospect that some day, most of these students at the raging end of the spectrum will be released. There are, after all, many people on the outside who I cherish, and many more, who I don't know, who are cherished by others. All of these people deserve to live in peace.

If our classrooms were composed only of those students at the far ends of the continuum—only of the irredeemable and the already redeemed—there would be precious little justification for paying our wages. The members of the former group are probably beyond cure, and the members of the latter group are probably already cured.

But then we come to the final group, the largest group along the continuum, the students who, upon their release, could go either way. Some will choose violence. Others will not. And there is a compelling statistical reason for providing these students with any and all kinds of education, including the exotic kind we call art.

Among the general prison population, the recidivism rate—that is, the rate at which former inmates reoffend and return to prison—runs at around 66 percent. But according to a study conducted by the National Institute of Criminal Justice—the research arm of the Justice Department—recidivism rates for those prisoners who complete a high school education while incarcerated drop to 45 percent. For those who complete a two-year college degree while inside, the rate drops to 27.5 percent. And inmates who acquire a four-year college degree while incarcerated, reoffend at a rate of 12 percent.

Statistics aside, if one of those students who could go either way gets out of prison and does *not* reoffend, it is impossible, of course, to pinpoint the cause. We can't attribute the former inmate's turn-around to Linda Waterfall's music, to Ernie Brown's firm but fair hand, or to Monda Van Hollabeck's patient, gentle teaching. We can't credit the Anger Management Program, or even the simple fact that as youthful fires begin to burn out at the age of thirty to thirty-five, some, but by no means all incarcerated individuals, begin to take a second look at their options.

I don't think anyone except, possibly, the former inmate in ques-tion, can explain why he turned away from violence. But we do know that somewhere out of the mix of non-punitive programs, a signifi-cant number of successes do emerge. And we know that when an in-mate signs up for an artist's residency, though he or she may not be signaling a full-fledged commitment to change, the inmate is signal-ing a willingness to try something new, to look at the world in a slightly different way, to expand his or her sense of possibilities; his or her sense of how to be in the world.

When I teach inside it is an all-consuming task for every participant, an outward bound of the soul. Every night my students and I go home with a thick stack of stories to be read by the next day. My stu-dents write and speak about their stories with a desperate edge that I've never encountered on the outside. As a teacher I become so ab-sorbed that I often forget—occasionally to my regret—that I'm teach-ing in a prison.

But when I leave my class for the final time, I am acutely aware where my students are staying, and why they are staying in prison. And during the ensuing few days I go over the roster again and again in the hope that I gave each student the love he deserved. For the abused, whipped puppies in class, it may have been respectful, dis-tant love. For the student who postures but doesn't really want to pos-ture, it may have been tough, in-your-face love. And for some, as with the Farrakhan supporter, it may have been copious amounts of pa-tient love.

I do this mental accounting in part because any group of stu-dents deserves its teacher's best. If I fell down, I want to correct my mistakes the next time. But I also do this accounting because there are, as I've said, many on the outside who I cherish; countless others who I don't know but who deserve to live in peace, and I would not want to see any of these people come to harm.

If I have done my job well enough, then, through the medium of story, all of my students will have realized that they have valid stories to tell by virtue of the fact that they're alive; most will have learned, in a visceral sense, about a new, non-violent way to channel rage, despair, and even joy; many students will have experienced the alchemy that takes place when the oft-sordid stuff of their lives is transformed into a gift, a story; some, I hope, will have found, if nothing else, a pleasant way to pass the time; and finally and most importantly, however indirect and incrementally, immersion in the artistic process will become one, among a number of factors, that will nudge one or two students toward a decision that will be made months or years down the line when they are back on the streets again: the decision to turn away from violence, to not hurt another human being.

   If the workshop has been instrumental in bringing about such a choice, then I have done my job. If it hasn't, then I have failed. Those are the stakes we're playing for in prison. It's really as simple as that.

About the Authors

Michael P. Collins was born in 1970. In 1988, at the age of eighteen, he was sentenced to serve eight years in Washington and ten years in Oregon on five counts of first degree armed robbery. He was paroled in 1997, and is currently working as a telephone cable installer. He is saving money to go to college.

Duane Eaglestaff was born in 1950. A twice-convicted rapist, he is currently being held at the Special Commitment Center under the auspices of Washington's Civil Commitment Law.

Jon Fleming was born in 1970. He is currently serving a twenty-year sentence at the Washington State Penitentiary in Walla Walla for two counts of first degree burglary, possession of a controlled substance, and unlawful possession of a firearm. Fleming has previously served time for multiple counts of burglary, possession of a controlled substance, and for assault. Fleming was first incarcerated as a juvenile at the age of fourteen. His adult record includes seventeen felony convictions.

TJ Granack was born in 1953. In 1982 he was sentenced to serve fifteen to thirty years for first degree attempted murder. He was paroled in 1994, and is currently working as a bartender.

Keith R. Lansdowne was born in 1960. He served twenty years for second degree murder and was released in September of 1998. He is currently training to become a long-haul truck driver.

Lesley Smith was born in 1956. He is currently serving a twenty-year sentence for first degree attempted murder.

Robert Ellis Gordon was born in 1954. He began teaching in the Washington State prisons in 1989. His award-winning novel, *When Bobby Kennedy Was a Moving Man*, was published by Black Heron Press in 1993. He has published stories and essays in numerous literary journals and magazines. Gordon was forced to stop teaching in prisons in the late 1990s because of draconian cuts in funding for prison education programs and because of his battle with advanced auto-immune disease.